Carol

Christmas 1998

IMAGES
of America

BRUNSWICK

A c. 1845 PAINTING, *EAGLE MILL*, ATTRIBUTED TO ARTIST THOMAS WILSON, ORIGINAL OWNED BY THE ABBEY ALDRICH ROCKEFELLER FOLK ART COLLECTION. The earliest known image of a Brunswick hamlet is this one of Eagle Mills, formerly Millville. The scene looks east from a point along present-day Pinewoods Avenue toward the Poestenkill Creek. The old Eagle Mills dam and a sawmill appear to the right. To the left of the bridge stands a four-story brick structure known then as the Eagle Mills where Eagle Brand Flour was produced. The mill complex later housed several other short-lived manufacturing ventures and is best remembered as the Planters's Hoe Company, founded *c.* 1854, which operated until 1907 despite several shutdowns and changes of ownership. (Courtesy Abbey Aldrich Rockefeller Folk Art Collection.)

IMAGES
of America

BRUNSWICK

*To Dr. John Coughlin,
Enjoy!
Sharon Martin Zankel
Dec 12, 1998*

Sharon Martin Zankel
for the Brunswick Historical Society

ARCADIA

Published by Arcadia Publishing,
an imprint of Tempus Publishing, Inc.
2 Cumberland Street
Charleston, SC 29401

Printed in Great Britain.

Library of Congress Catalog Card Number: 98-87782

For all general information contact Arcadia Publishing at:
Telephone 843-853-2070
Fax 843-853-0044
E-Mail arcadia@charleston.net

For customer service and orders:
Toll-Free 1-888-313-BOOK

Visit us on the internet at http://www.arcadiaimages.com

In memory of Amanda Gibbs (1983–1996).
This work is dedicated to the children of Brunswick that they may
appreciate and enjoy our local heritage.

AMANDA GIBBS (CENTER), HER PLAYMATE LINDSEY, AND THE AUTHOR'S DOG, HEIDI, ON A SUNNY AUTUMN AFTERNOON, 1990. This image appeared in the Brunswick Historical Society's 1990 video production *Brunswick . . . Our Town, Our Heritage.* On another day, Amanda helped put together an exhibit of old photographs and commented the pictures should be put in a book so she could show them to her friends. (Photograph by Sharon Martin Zankel.)

CONTENTS

SCHOOL DISTRICT NO. 2, THE 1881 GARFIELD SCHOOL, 605 BRUNSWICK ROAD (ROUTE 2), EAGLE MILLS, PHOTOGRAPHED C. 1881. This two-room school became known as the Garfield School in recognition of Pres. James A. Garfield who, in the 1850s, taught at an earlier Eagle Mills schoolhouse while attending Williams College. The Garfield School closed in the 1960s. In 1986 the school was conveyed to the Town of Brunswick by the Brittonkill School District with a deed restriction that it be used for educational purposes. The Brunswick Historical Society long supported restoration and reuse of the schoolhouse and was granted use of half the building as an exhibition and meeting space. The other half was reserved for a community library formed in 1988, now the Garfield Library of Brunswick. The Garfield School is listed on the National Register of Historic Places. (Brunswick Historical Society Collection.)

INTRODUCTION

The refinement of photography during the mid- to late 1800s added a new and exciting dimension to the recording as well as the collection of history. The photographers of the mid-1800s concentrated on the creation of lifelike portraits that would keep one's image alive long after the spirit had departed this life. Later, the exhibition of the images, by photographers such as Mathew Brady, produced during the Civil War revealed the camera's ability to communicate a sense of being at the scene of the action.

As late-19th-century photographers expanded their subject matter to include anything from commanding landscape scenes to poignant pictures of unfortunate social conditions, it was realized a photograph could arouse a viewer's emotions, concerns, and reactions as well as illustrate history. The uses for photographs and the opportunities for photographers quickly multiplied, encouraging the simplification of the camera and its operation. By the early 20th century, many people were collecting photographs; some owned cameras or knew someone who did. Our fascination with old photographs is, in this work, with the images as a medium for recovering, exploring, and experiencing our community's past.

This collection of photographs offers a pictorial journey through Brunswick, New York, from about 1880 to 1970. In 1978, the Brunswick Historical Society published the early history of Brunswick, from its settlement c. 1720 through 1910, in the book *Brunswick . . . A Pictorial History*, edited by Warren Broderick and now out-of-print. The present work offers those who missed the earlier publication an opportunity to enjoy a few of the only known photographs of certain vintage scenes. Most of the photographs presented herein, however, have never before been published. This work is divided into eight thematic chapters. The first chapter, "Historic Sights," includes roadside scenes intended to present a cumulative image of Brunswick at the beginning of the 20th century. The remainder of the book focuses on those who have shaped the history of our town—our people. The homes, organizations, and businesses our citizens built and the values and traditions they shared are illustrated through these photographs, many created by those citizens. The third chapter, "Remembering Our Youth," and the fifth chapter, "School Days," are especially intended for the enjoyment of young readers.

Located in Rensselaer County, New York, the town of Brunswick is east of the city of Troy, from which it was formed by an act of the New York State Legislature on March 20, 1807. Previously, from the time of the Revolution until Rensselaer County was organized in 1791, the area today known as Brunswick was in the town of Rensselaerwyck, Albany County. While a lengthy report of Brunswick's history as a part of Rensselaerwyck is not appropriate in this summary, readers may wish to consult Nathaniel Sylvester's *History of Rensselaer County* (1880) or George B. Anderson's *Landmarks of Rensselaer County, New York* (1897) for a study of this fascinating era in our local past.

Comprising an area of about 48 square miles, the town of Brunswick has no cities or villages.

Its current population is estimated to be 13,500, nearly 10,000 more than lived here at the close of the 19th century. The histories cited above identify the hamlets today known as Center Brunswick (then Brunswick Centre), Eagle Mills (formerly Millville), Cropseyville, Clum's Corners, Haynersville (then Haynerville), and Tamarac (formerly Platestown) as Brunswick's then-significant settlements. No mention is made of the neighborhoods Mountain View and Sycaway, both situated on the Brunswick-Troy line and now the most urban areas of the town, as their identities by these names had not then been established.

Brunswick has a long history as a farming community. The earliest settlers leased their lands from the patroon of VanRensselaer Manor primarily for the purpose of establishing farms. The area's fertile soil and close proximity to Troy encouraged many to settle here. Initially grain, then produce such as potatoes, were sold in Troy or shipped from Troy to distant locations. As the industrial city of Troy grew, Brunswick farmers found it to be a lucrative market for milk and other dairy products, fresh garden produce, and hay for the bedding of horses. While the number of farms in Brunswick has declined considerably over the last 30 years, Brunswick yet hosts several large dairy operations, one—the Herrington Farm in Tamarac—producing more milk than any other in the county. In the last decade, several farmers have abandoned dairy farming, turning to the production of grain or raising beef cattle and, now, "organically" grown produce. Brunswick's history as an agricultural community continues to evolve.

A part of Brunswick's history often overlooked is its early industrial economy. The energy of the town's major streams, the Poestenkill and Quackenkill Creeks, sparked the growth of numerous mills and factories at Eagle Mills and Cropseyville. It has been advanced by earlier writers that the first gristmill in Rensselaer County was erected in Cropseyville, perhaps as early as 1772. Gristmills, sawmills, a foundry, and numerous factories producing goods no longer familiar to us encouraged the growth of the hamlets Eagle Mills and Cropseyville. Obsolescence, fire, bankruptcy, the lack of rail service, and, in the case of Cropseyville, the diversion of water from the Quackenkill to Lape's Lake, then a part of Troy's water supply, were several of the factors that brought about the demise of the town's waterpowered industries. The passage of time has erased almost all evidence of these 19th-century enterprises.

The compilation of this pictorial history would not have been possible without the photograph collections of the Brunswick Historical Society and the Town of Brunswick, and the generous loan of many images by townspeople. Special recognition is due the many historical society members who have donated, collected, preserved, and identified the hundreds of photographs in the society's archives over the years. Much appreciation is also extended to former Brunswick Town Historians Florence Carner Lee and Dorothy Ives McChesney, for their efforts in creating and preserving the Town of Brunswick's photograph collection. Jeanne B. Jarrett, Donald and Helen Clickner, Irene Miller, Mildred McChesney, Eleanor Hill, George and Eleanor Reckner, Donald Patton, and Fred Schafer are among the many who offered much helpful information. Recognition is given Harold Ashdown, who arranged the loan of many photographs by townspeople and assisted with taping oral histories associated with some of the images. Thanks, too, to Ned Pratt, director of the Shaker Heritage Society in Albany, New York, who provided editorial assistance. The Rensselaer County Historical Society in Troy, The New York State Library in Albany, the Abbey Aldrich Rockefeller Folk Art Collection of Colonial Williamsburg, and the publishers of *The Record*, Troy, are thanked for their permission to include images owned by them.

I especially thank my husband, Lewis, and parents, Les and Clara Martin, for their never-ending support of my work on this project, and my friend, Karen Hartgen Fisher, North Greenbush Town Historian, for her ongoing encouragement.

Now, please enjoy this pictorial journey through Brunswick!

Sharon Martin Zankel
Eagle Mills, Brunswick, New York
July 1998

One
HISTORIC SIGHTS

JUNCTION OF THE STONE ROAD, NOW HOOSICK ROAD (ROUTE 7), LEFT, WITH THE BRICK CHURCH ROAD, ROUTE 278, C. 1915. The Stone Road, known earlier as the McAdam Road, closely follows the path of the ancient Hosek Road, the first public highway to traverse the area that would become Rensselaer County in 1791. The view here is toward Haynersville, where German Palatines settled c. 1720 and, by 1742, founded the Gilead Lutheran Church. Pictured is the fourth and present Gilead house of worship. At the time of this photograph and until the 1960s, the brick church was painted a buff color. The house on the old Sheffer Farm, in the foreground, may be readily recognized today although it is used for professional offices. It has been said many who passed through this area in the stagecoaches of yesterday were much attracted to Brunswick's scenic beauty and returned to settle here. (Brunswick Historical Society Collection.)

THE GILEAD LUTHERAN CHURCH, BUILT 1865, 308 BRICK CHURCH ROAD. In 1818 the Gilead congregation moved from Haynersville, where it built its first two churches, to its current location. The first church erected on this site was dedicated in 1818. This photograph of the present church was taken shortly after its construction during the Civil War. In 1892, the spires were replaced with ornamental iron cresting (see p. 9). The family names of many of the early settlers of the local area may be found in the records of the Gilead church. (Brunswick Historical Society Collection.)

A GILEAD CHURCH WOMEN'S GROUP. Church-related activities and gatherings provided social outlets while furthering the endurance of the religious order. A group photograph with friends and neighbors aside one's church was surely a treasured memento. The plaque by the church's entrance indicates John Weaver was then pastor and places the date of the photograph between 1888 and 1912, the period of his service. The plaque also indicates Mason Undertakers of Lansingburgh provided undertaking services, and that Mathias Semback was the sexton. (Courtesy Ray Shaver.)

A CENTER BRUNSWICK STREET SCENE, HOOSICK ROAD (ROUTE 7) AND GRANGE ROAD (ROUTE 142), C. 1910. The home of Joe and Edith Coonrad is to the right. Joe (see p. 102) remodeled the home, adding ornamental woodwork he had crafted on a foot-peddled jigsaw. Next to the Coonrad home was Joe's blacksmith shop (see p. 111). A hall above the shop provided meeting space for community groups. Joe later converted the shop into an automotive repair shop and gas station. The structure past Coonrad's shop housed a harness shop operated by Hiram Littlefield, owner of the building, and a general store operated by Ernest Brust and Herbert Hayner. The house across from Littlefield's was once the home and grocery store of Michael and Emily Jane Coonradt. Littlefield's building is the only one that yet stands at this site and has been converted to apartments. (Town of Brunswick Collection.)

THE CENTRE HOUSE, CENTER BRUNSWICK, AT THE INTERSECTION OF SWEET MILK CREEK, GRANGE, AND HOOSICK ROADS, C. 1912. Once described as the site of "bustling scenes by day and revelry by night," this early tavern conveyed a lonesome appearance when photographed shortly before it was dismantled to be rebuilt as a barn in Melrose. Thought to be about 150 years old at the time it was razed, the hotel was originally built to provide stagecoach travelers rest and refreshment. The building was nicknamed the "soup house" in the 1880s when it served as a distribution point of soup for the needy. (Town of Brunswick Collection.)

WHITE'S HOTEL, FORMERLY LUCAS BROWN'S ROADHOUSE, HOOSICK ROAD (ROUTE 7), EARLY 1900s. White's Hotel is the first building to the left but the picture also provides a bygone view of the present Route 7 commercial district, looking east from the Midas Muffler Shop that now stands on the site of the old hotel. The annual "town meeting" of Brunswick was held at hotels such as this one. In the early 1900s, the hotel was converted to an apartment house. It was destroyed by fire in 1941. The home once occupied by Herbert Hasbrouck is next to the hotel; beyond that was the farm of Carroll Herrington. (Town of Brunswick Collection.)

THE BRUNSWICK METHODIST EPISCOPAL
CHURCH, BUILT 1835, NOW THE SITE OF
BRUNSWICK HARLEY-DAVIDSON, INC.,
ROUTE 7. The Brunswick Episcopal
Church was organized the same year it
built this church. The bell tower was added
in 1866 and, according to church records,
was the only church bell in town at the
time (there were then four churches in
Brunswick). This church was torn down in
1902 and its timbers used for framing a new
church, pictured below, about a mile west
of this site. (Courtesy Eleanor Wilson.)

THE CENTER BRUNSWICK METHODIST CHURCH AND PARSONAGE, HOOSICK ROAD (ROUTE
7) AT GRANGE ROAD, PHOTOGRAPHED C. 1916. This parsonage, razed in 1994, predated the
church next to it and was constructed over a period of three years, beginning in 1872. The
construction costs were shared by the Center Brunswick, Eagle Mills, and East Brunswick
Methodist Churches as they then shared the pastor's services. The new church was dedicated
April 22, 1903. Churchgoers parked their horses and buggies in the carriage sheds seen in the
background. In 1953, the bell from the first church, above, was sold and replaced by organ
chimes. (Brunswick Historical Society Collection.)

PICNICKERS, MOUNT RAFINESQUE, COMMONLY KNOWN AS BALD MOUNTAIN, OCTOBER 2, 1892. These unknown individuals are having a good laugh while enjoying the last picnic of the season. Generally referred to as Bald Mountain because of its exposed rocky summits, this landmark officially took the name of the French scientist Constantine Rafinesque, who studied plant life here about 1833. (Courtesy Warren Broderick.)

THE INTERIOR OF LAFLEURS HALL, MOUNTAIN VIEW, EARLY 1900S. About 1910, the Mountain View Republican Club was formed and built a meeting hall, later known as LaFleurs Hall and, next, as the Mountain View Community Center. In 1945, the building was demolished for the construction of the Mountain View fire station. The sign indicates the hall's location is Albia (an adjacent neighborhood in the city of Troy), an indication that Brunswick neighborhoods along the Troy city line established an identity with that municipality. (Courtesy Mountain View Volunteer Fire Department.)

14

THE TOLLGATE AND COVERED
BRIDGE, POESTENKILL CREEK,
LOOKING EAST ALONG PRESENT-DAY
BRUNSWICK ROAD (ROUTE 2),
FORMERLY THE PITTSTOWN
TURNPIKE, TOWARD SHIPPEY LANE
AND EAGLE MILLS, C. 1870. This
turnpike was, like the Stone Road
(Route 7), a toll road and was
maintained by a private company.
The tollgate, at what later became
known as White Bridge, was
associated with a covered bridge that
went down in an 1892 flood. The
tollgate earlier stood near the old
Colehamer Farm west of this site.
(Town of Brunswick Collection.)

THE "PAINT FACTORY" DAM, POESTENKILL CREEK, WEST OF EAGLE MILLS. Little is known
about the industry that sparked the construction of this dam along the Poestenkill. It has been
said a paint factory once existed at the end of the road now known as Cole Lane. Workers
chipped shale from the ledges along the creek and transported it down the creek in a scow to
the factory where it was ground for the manufacture of red paint. Several recall exploring the
ruins of the dam in the 1930s. The story of its beginnings was passed down by their fathers and
grandfathers to them. (Courtesy Donald Patton.)

REV. E.J. BUTLER AND CHOIR, CHURCH OF CHRIST, DISCIPLES, CORNER OF BRUNSWICK ROAD (ROUTE 2) AND MAPLE AVENUE, EAGLE MILLS, C. 1901. This congregation was organized in 1852 and the church was built in 1853. James A. Garfield preached several sermons here during the 1850s. The choir members in this photograph, attributed to Andrew Mullin (see p. 98), are, from left to right, Gertrude Rowe Martin, Anna Tamm Lynd, Nina Band Miller, Isabelle Rowe Shaver, Florence Mullin Reed (Andrew's daughter), and Sarah Campbell Sullivan. On May 7, 1911, the church, along with more than a dozen other structures in the hamlet of Eagle Mills, was destroyed by a fire caused by the explosion of a gasoline heater while water was being heated in the baptistery. (Town of Brunswick Collection.)

LOOKING WEST FROM THE EAGLE MILLS BRIDGE, INTERSECTION OF PINEWOODS AVENUE, FORMERLY KNOWN AS THE OLD ROAD, AND BRUNSWICK ROAD (ROUTE 2), EAGLE MILLS, C. 1900. This photograph is taken from a postcard. To the far right is the structure occupied by the Planters's Hoe Company, once an around-the-clock operation and a major employer in late-19th-century Brunswick. The home at the center of the picture was that of Peter VanZandt. About 1931, with the widening of the road that would become Route 2, the VanZandt home was moved back and the shoemaker's shop to the right of VanZandt's was relocated. The Joseph Lee family (see p. 46) later acquired the VanZandt home and built a dairy here. (Brunswick Historical Society Collection.)

THE RUINS LEFT BY THE 1911 FIRE THAT STARTED IN THE CHURCH OF CHRIST, EAGLE MILLS. The photographer viewed this scene of the fire's aftermath from the northeast bank of the Poestenkill Creek. The Planters's Hoe Company, once known as the Eagle Mills (see p. 2) and from which the hamlet ultimately received its name, stands in ruins, never to be rebuilt as it had terminated manufacturing operations several years before this conflagration. (Brunswick Historical Society Collection.)

THE SECOND CHURCH OF CHRIST, DISCIPLES, EAGLE MILLS, BUILT 1912. Following the destruction of the first church, steps were immediately taken to erect a new church on the same site. The new church was dedicated on October 12, 1912. In 1976, the Church of Christ at Eagle Mills disbanded and its building was conveyed to the Church of Christ, Scientist. (Town of Brunswick Collection.)

THE EAGLE MILLS IRON BRIDGE AND SHIRT FACTORY, FROM A POSTCARD POSTMARKED 1906.
A shirt factory was operated by Louis Thurston in the structure adjacent to the bridge, on the corner of Brunswick and Creek Roads. Other shirt factories in Brunswick included Smith's in Cropseyville, Deemer's in Tamarac, and Brust's in Center Brunswick. Brunswick's close proximity to Troy also encouraged the manufacturers there to rely on local women to turn collars and stitch buttonholes in their homes. The work was delivered in baskets and left at the doorstep, the general store, or post office. The women were paid a piecework rate, several cents for each dozen articles completed. (Courtesy Lewis Zankel.)

A WOMAN DRIVING A HORSE AND BUGGY ALONG CREEK ROAD, SOUTH OF EAGLE MILLS. This lone traveler has paused momentarily to enjoy a tranquil moment along the Poestenkill Creek. Scattered leaves along the roadside indicate the arrival of early autumn. The name Poestenkill is of Dutch origin signifying a "puffing or foaming creek," a characteristic of the stream not obvious in this view. (Town of Brunswick Collection.)

POESTENKILL CREEK AND THE DAM AT EAGLE MILLS. In this image the icy waters of the Poestenkill have recently taken out the eastern end of the Eagle Mills dam on their way to join the Hudson River at Troy. The scene encourages our realization of the power of the stream that supported many early industries in Poestenkill, Eagle Mills, and Troy. The old McChesney sawmill, one of several enterprises that harnessed the creek's power at Eagle Mills, appears to the left. The men standing behind the mill are examining the damage to the dam. About 1927, the remainder of the dam was demolished when a dispute among local folks over ice-cutting rights on the millpond was settled by dynamite rather than negotiation. The dam was never restored as all the waterpowered industries at Eagle Mills had by then disappeared. A more poignant incident relating to the dam occurred in 1885 when Mahala Smith Jones was hurled to her death as her boat slipped over the edge of the dam while she was gathering driftwood for fuel. (Town of Brunswick Collection.)

HOOK'S BLACKSMITH SHOP, NOW 537 BRUNSWICK ROAD, EAGLE MILLS, C. 1880. Andrew Mullin (see p. 98) photographed the Hook family in front of the business founded by John M. Hook. Upon his death in 1899, the business was carried on by his son, John J. Hook (1873–1951), assisted by a brother, William. In 1936, John J. Hook, noting the declining need for blacksmiths, invited all of Rensselaer County's remaining "smithies" to his home for dinner; his guests numbered 20. Upon his passing, John J. Hook was eulogized as the "dean of blacksmiths." The building was nearly destroyed by fire in 1990 but has been rebuilt. (Town of Brunswick Collection.)

VANZANDT'S STORE, EAGLE MILLS, BUILT 1888. Located next to Hook's blacksmith shop, this building has hosted a succession of business ventures. Andrew Mullin operated the store on behalf of Mr. VanZandt and eventually purchased the building. He also ran a small post office here. About 1924, John Dixon and Charles Rifenburg (see p. 93) formed a partnership and purchased the store with Dixon assuming full ownership shortly thereafter. The old building housed a barbershop, run first by Charles Butler (see p. 98) and subsequently by John Rube. A second-story meeting room and theatre once hosted concerts and other community events. (Brunswick Historical Society Collection.)

THE EAGLE MILLS HOTEL, EAGLE MILLS. This hotel, across from VanZandt's store, was operated by a number of innkeepers throughout the 19th century and was under the proprietorship of J. McMahon at the time of this photograph. The building is decorated for the celebration of Independence Day. Later images (see below and p. 57) indicate the old hotel was remodeled several times. About 1932, Harold and Grace Winne opened an ice cream parlor here. Next it became a store. The building burned after a tanning salon opened here in 1993 and was so extensively damaged it had to be demolished. (Town of Brunswick Collection.)

LOOKING EAST ALONG BRUNSWICK ROAD (ROUTE 2) FROM THE EAGLE MILLS CONCRETE BRIDGE, C. 1940. Construction of a concrete bridge to replace the iron bridge over the Poestenkill in 1923 was much debated as its anticipated $6,000 cost would require issuing bonds. The bonds were issued but the actual cost of the bridge was $8,000! While the new bridge was under construction, a pontoon bridge was erected south of the old bridge. Hook's blacksmith shop and VanZandt's store, left, and the old Eagle Mills Hotel, right, display updated looks. (Brunswick Historical Society Collection.)

THE EAGLE MILLS METHODIST CHURCH, CORNER OF BRUNSWICK ROAD (ROUTE 2), LOOKING SOUTH ALONG GARFIELD ROAD. This photograph is from a postcard. The congregation was founded in 1849 and dedicated this church the next year. In 1903, the church was enlarged. The sanctuary pictured here was a new addition while the second floor of the original church was lowered, repositioned, and placed to the rear. In 1973, the congregation moved to a new church at 566 Brunswick Road and this building was subsequently razed. The home behind the church was once a tourist home known as the Blue Spruce. (Brunswick Historical Society Collection.)

WESLEY HOUSE, EAGLE MILLS, C. 1970. The McChesney/Dunham/Darrow home stood west of the Eagle Mills Methodist Church (pictured at the top of the page), and was acquired by the Church in 1956 to accommodate Sunday school classes and youth activities. It was named Wesley House. The building was later moved south of its original location to permit construction of the new Eagle Mills Methodist Church, now Hope United Methodist Church, and again serves as a private residence on the street now known as Parsonage Lane. (Courtesy Mr. and Mrs. Donald Clickner.)

THE CAMP OF THE 15TH U.S. CAVALRY, EAGLE MILLS, C. 1906, FROM A POSTCARD. This troop was en route from Fort Ethan Allen in Vermont to Mount Gretna, PA, to participate in joint army-militia maneuvers. The cavalrymen spent an afternoon and night camped on the property of Louis Thurston, near the Poestenkill Creek. One local resident today recalls his father describing this sight as being quite impressive. (Courtesy Sharon Martin Zankel.)

THE FIRST PRESBYTERIAN CHURCH OF BRUNSWICK, ALSO KNOWN AS THE WHITE CHURCH, WHITE CHURCH LANE. This photograph appeared on the church's 1959 sesquicentennial celebration program. The organizers of the First Presbyterian Church of Brunswick first met in 1809. In 1812 services were conducted in the newly built church although the pulpit had not yet been completed. In 1861, the church, except for the frame, was torn down and reconstructed. Whenever it is asked why the First Presbyterian Church of Brunswick is referred to as "the White Church," the usual response is, " Because it has always been painted white!" (Brunswick Historical Society Collection.)

Post office Cropseyville

THE CROPSEYVILLE POST OFFICE, C. 1910. The first Cropseyville Post Office opened in 1854. Following the Civil War, the post office was situated in this building, the home and harness shop of Richard Hulbert, who served as postmaster from 1889 until his death in 1899. His daughter, Clara Hulbert, succeeded him as postmistress, serving about 50 years. Miss Hulbert provided postal patrons rocking chairs and magazines in the event a wait was required. To the right of the post office was the Bennett brothers' shoe manufactory and repair shop. (Courtesy Mildred McChesney.)

A CROPSEYVILLE STREET SCENE, 1920s. The view is from Route 2 toward Clum's Corners. The frame structure in the left foreground was associated with a mill complex (see p. 25) and displays a circus advertisement. Next on the left is the first Odd Fellows Hall. To the right is the building known first as Valentine Cropsey's Hall, a community meeting place; it was later used as a boardinghouse for mill workers and called the "beehive." Next on the right are the Hulbert home and post office and, in the distance, the Newbury home. (Courtesy Iola Simmons.)

CROPSEYVILLE MILLS, C. 1910. This view looks along Route 2 from its junction with Bulson Road toward Clum's Corners. Pictured are Herman Brust and his son Harry alongside the gristmill that was owned and operated by the Cropsey family (for whom the hamlet was named) from about 1810 until 1866, when it was acquired by Reuben Smith. Reuben's son Paul expanded and improved the mill with borrowed capital, making it "the best in this section of the state" by 1890. Brust was one of several who owned the mill after a series of unfortunate events forced Paul into bankruptcy. The mill was demolished about 1950. (Town of Brunswick Collection.)

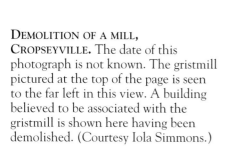

DEMOLITION OF A MILL, CROPSEYVILLE. The date of this photograph is not known. The gristmill pictured at the top of the page is seen to the far left in this view. A building believed to be associated with the gristmill is shown here having been demolished. (Courtesy Iola Simmons.)

MORRISON'S BRIDGE, CROPSEYVILLE, N.Y.

MORRISON'S BRIDGE AND THE MORRISON HOME, ROUTE 2, EAST OF BULSON ROAD, CROPSEYVILLE, C. 1900. Four generations of the Morrison family lived on the farm pictured here. The house was built in the 1790s by Henry Morrison and was last occupied by Brigham Morrison and his wife, Emma Coonrad, about 1941. Many of the Morrison family who resided here rest in the cemetery on a hillside overlooking the farm. (Courtesy Mildred McChesney.)

JOHN BOTT'S BLACKSMITH SHOP, EAST OF BULSON ROAD, ON ROUTE 2, C. 1900. This was formerly the Rockenstyre blacksmith shop where, in one week in 1890, 127 horses and 9 yoke of oxen were shod. In the 1920s, John Bott closed the business and went to work in Troy. The Bott home, surrounded by a white picket fence, can be seen to the left. (Courtesy Mildred McChesney.)

26

THE MCCHESNEY-GREEN MILL, ERECTED C. 1790, CROPSEYVILLE. Located east of South Road along the Quackenkill, this structure was originally built by Walter D. McChesney as a sawmill and was later operated by Job Green first as a woolen mill and then as a gristmill. A dam once stood several hundred feet from the mill on the Quackenkill Creek. Although much of the original structure has been replaced, its original floors and framing remain intact. This is the only surviving building associated with Brunswick's many early waterpowered industries. (Brunswick Historical Society Collection.)

THE PLEASANT VALLEY STORE, EAST OF CROPSEYVILLE, C. 1910. Built and operated as a hotel at the eastern end of Cropseyville, then known as Rock Hollow, Edward McChesney acquired this building in 1886 and converted it to a general store. The store was called the Pleasant Valley Store, a name by which the neighborhood soon became known. The store was acquired by Charles Rifenburg in 1905 (see p. 93). Broadsides advertising Kemp's Balsam and Lane's Medicine indicate these were of two of the commodities sold here. (Brunswick Historical Society Collection.)

A POSTCARD SCENE TITLED "BIRDS EYE VIEW OF CLUM'S CORNERS," C. 1912. The view is toward Clum's Flats, in the center of the photograph, from Brick Church Road (Route 278). Local residents once raced their horses on Clum's Flats on Sunday afternoons. Today, the Brittonkill School occupies the area to the left behind the first row of trees; the Tamarac Plaza and several commercial establishments have been constructed in the area to the right. The District No. 6 schoolhouse appears in the foreground to the right. (Brunswick Historical Society Collection.)

A POSTCARD SCENE OF THE JUNCTION OF ROUTE 278 AND TAMARAC ROAD, CLUM'S CORNERS, C. 1912. Clum's blacksmith shop is on the left. One of the men pictured may be Orlin J. Clum (born 1845), the son of James Clum and Christina Brust. Orlin's father was also a blacksmith. The automobile bears a 1912 Massachusetts license plate. The view looks toward Tamarac Road. The advertisement painted on the barn behind the waiting team of horses cannot be discerned. (Brunswick Historical Society Collection.)

Two

OUT OUR WAY

THE TAMM FAMILY AND HOME, 391 CREEK ROAD, EAGLE MILLS, C. 1913. Ernest Tamm (1858–1941) came to this area from Germany at about age 20; he married Minnie Knebush (1861–1935). Their children were Ernest Jr., Robert, William, Edward, and Anna. One Tamm family legend is that Edward could write with either hand. Here, Minnie and Ernest Sr. stand on the steps to the right. Anna is behind the wheel of a Ford convertible with kerosene headlamps. The two men to the left of Anna may be two of her brothers. The car's windshield was folded down to photograph its occupants. Through the study of old photographs, we learn how people lived, worked, and played. Family legends, values, and traditions become a part of our shared local heritage. (Courtesy Marion Lynd.)

THOMAS PATTON (1807–1890). Thomas Patton, born in Troy, was the son of Alexander Patton (born 1779 in Scotland, died 1828) and Ann DeWitt VanWagoner (1783–1850). In 1841, Thomas purchased a farm in Brunswick, seen below. He also engaged in the leather business in Troy. He married Drusilla Gorton in 1831. (Courtesy Donald Patton.)

THE PATTON FARM, 250 PINEWOODS AVENUE, C. 1960. The barn, built in 1914 by Alton File of Cropseyville, replaced an earlier structure that burned when struck by lightening. A railroad car of slate was required to build the barn's roof. Alexander Patton, the son of Thomas and Drusilla, built another home west of this one. (Courtesy Donald Patton.)

DRUSILLA GORTON PATTON,
(1808–1867). Drusilla Gorton, the
daughter of Benjamin and Polly Foster
Gorton, was born in Troy and married
Thomas Patton (see p. 30). They had nine
children, but only seven survived infancy:
James G., George H., Mary D., Sarah L.,
Anna J., Francis T., and Alexander G.
(Courtesy Donald Patton.)

ALEXANDER GORTON PATTON,
(1837–1919). Alexander, the youngest child
of Thomas and Drusilla Patton, was born in
Troy. He and his first wife, Emma Gorton
(1836–1874), had four children but none
survived childhood. Alexander's second wife,
Sarah Jane Ives (1845–1929), bore one son,
Thomas, in 1880 (see p. 122). Alexander
managed the family farm following the death
of his father and purchased it from his father's
estate in 1890 for his son to operate.
Alexander served as a first lieutenant with
the Black Horse Cavalry at Camp Strong
during the Civil War. (Courtesy Donald
Patton.)

TARGET FARM, DEARSTYNE ROAD, C. 1920. This photograph was probably taken when Phillip P. Pollock owned this property. He sold it to Herbert Hayner, who subsequently conveyed it to Phillip's brother, Fred Pollock. Fred started calling the place Target Farm when dissension among several members of a nearby sportsman's club created a new target range in a field near the farm. (Courtesy Phil Pollock.)

WELCH FARM, 414 BRUNSWICK ROAD (ROUTE 2), EAGLE MILLS. This property photographed in the late 1800s, was acquired by Edward Welch, grandfather of its current owner, James P. "Jay" Welch, in 1905. The house was destroyed by fired about 1931 and a new home was constructed on the same foundation. The horse-drawn conveyance to the right is a funeral hearse but its association with the farm is not known. It has been suggested a local undertaker may have used one of the barns for storage of the hearse. (Courtesy Jay Welch.)

32

THE HOME AT 446 McChesney Avenue Extension, c. 1910. Wilson Wagar and his wife, Effie Clickner, purchased this home, formerly that of Charles M. and Adelia (Coons) Potter, sometime after their marriage in 1902. Pictured, from left to right, are an unidentified person, Wilson Wagar, Pearl Rose, Emma Wagar, and Effie Wagar. Emma, the daughter of Wilson and Effie, married Francis J. Flynn. The home is now owned by their descendants. (Courtesy Margaret Flynn.)

THE Coonradt-Mayer home, 468 McChesney Avenue Extension, built c. 1863. This home has changed little since Ethel Miller (see p. 46) took this picture about 1920 while the house was owned by her uncle, Charles Mayer. The current owner's research of the history of the house indicates it was first occupied by the David H. Coonradt family. (Photograph by Ethel Miller; courtesy Irene Miller.)

THE JOHN MCCHESNEY HOME, 126 MCCHESNEY AVENUE. Tennette McChesney (1851–1932) stands to the left behind the picket fence. Her mother, Christina, is seated to the right. The man holding the horses may be Dallas Wagar, who boarded with the family. Tennette was born and died in this home, built in 1805 by her father, John McChesney. A hammock has been strung between two trees and a rocking chair placed on the porch, indicating the family enjoyed outdoor relaxation during the summer. (Brunswick Historical Society Collection.)

PLAYING CROQUET AT THE DERRICK HOME, 936 HOOSICK ROAD, C. 1900. The lawn game croquet was introduced in the United States about 1870 and remained popular for several decades. Playing the game on a bygone day are, from left to right, Olive St. John, Beulah Derrick, and Mary St. John. The Federal-period home was probably constructed in the early 1800s and was long in the Derrick family. The Gummer, Keyes, and Bonesteel families were among this property's later owners. (Brunswick Historical Society Collection.)

THE RICHARD A. DERRICK HOME, ROUTE 7 AT SPRINGBROOK ROAD. This photograph is from a 1947 Christmas greeting sent by Francis and Mary O'Brien, who then owned the property. The farm consisted of about 400 acres and was once occupied by Richard A. Derrick (see p. 99). After the sale of the property by the O'Brien family, much of the acreage was divided into building lots for the residential area developed around Springbrook Road. (Courtesy John and Joann Tarbox.)

THE FILE HOME, BUILT C. 1791, HOOSICK ROAD (ROUTE 7) BETWEEN CENTER BRUNSWICK AND HAYNERSVILLE. About 1761, John Melchoir File and his wife, Elizabeth Rickert Hunsinger, moved to Brunswick, then a part of the Dutch estate known as Rensselaerwyck, and rented 232 acres of land. Like many German immigrants, John's sympathies were with the Loyalists during the American Revolution. He fought with the British at the Battle of Saratoga and, after their defeat, guided many loyalists to Canada. While many loyalists from Brunswick remained in Canada, John File stayed in Brunswick, although he was fined and punished several times. (Photograph by Sharon Martin Zankel.)

THE FILIEAU HOME, 734 PINEWOODS AVENUE, EAGLE MILLS, BUILT C. 1876. Joachim Filieau built this home and resided here with his family until about 1891. The next occupants were Brainard and Cornelia Link. When the Links separated, the home was rented to Minerva Sweet (see p. 37). In 1912, it was sold to Dr. Porter Oakley, a Troy dentist, who used it as a summer residence. Roy and Anna Hulett acquired the house in 1929 and lived here for 40 years. (Photograph by Sharon Martin Zankel.)

JOACHIM FILIEAU (1839–1916) AND WIFE, MARIETTA (1839–1919). Joachim was born in Canada where he studied for the priesthood. Sometime before the Civil War, he relocated to Connecticut, where he married Marietta and enlisted in the 11th Connecticut Volunteers in 1861. After the Civil War, Joachim and Marietta settled in Eagle Mills. Joachim worked at the Planter's Hoe Company as a carpenter. He later built the Garfield School (see p. 6) and VanZandt's store (see p. 20). (Town of Brunswick Collection.)

THE DATER HOME, 567 BRUNSWICK ROAD, EAGLE MILLS, BUILT C. 1798. This home was originally owned by James and Mary Cox, who conveyed the house to Philip P. Dater, a veteran of the War of 1812. The house remained in the Dater family until 1899 and has passed through a number of owners in the 20th century, including the Lohnes, Abbott, Thurston, Sweet, Wood, and Redick families. (Brunswick Historical Society Collection.)

MINERVA SWEET (1864–1945) AND HER SONS, WILLIAM YOURT SWEET (1899–1974), CENTER, AND ROGER (1901–1962). This family moved from the Filieau house to the Dater house. Minerva was the wife of William A. Sweet. Roger Sweet became a popular singer, performing on radio station WGY. He was later a music librarian, residing in New York City. William worked for several local industries. He and his wife, Helen, while living at the Dater house, sometimes rented rooms to tourists. (Courtesy Bill Sweet.)

DR. CORNELIUS A. WINSHIP (1826–1888), LEFT, AND TWO OF HIS CONTEMPORARIES, GEORGE MORRISON, CENTER, AND HIRAM McCHESNEY. Dr. C.A. Winship came to Eagle Mills from Litchfield, Connecticut. He maintained an office in his home where he was known to perform surgery when necessary. His first wife was Helen Kimberly; after her death, he married Sarah Band. (Courtesy Elizabeth Winship Nicoll.)

THE WINSHIP HOME, 718 PINEWOODS AVENUE, EAGLE MILLS, BUILT C. 1857. This house served as the residence and office of Dr. Cornelius Winship and, later, his son, Dr. Frank Winship. The four Tuscan columns on the front of the house were manufactured in Mt. Vernon, New York, and were transported to Albany by rail and from there to Eagle Mills by horse-drawn conveyance when the house was remodeled in 1904. The house remains in the Winship family. (Courtesy Elizabeth Winship Nicoll.)

HELEN KIMBERLY WINSHIP (1831–1876). Helen was the first wife of Dr. Cornelius Winship and the mother of two sons, David (1853–1926) and Frank, pictured at the bottom of this page. (Courtesy Elizabeth Winship Nicoll.)

DR. FRANK WINSHIP (1863–1945), SON OF DR. CORNELIUS AND HELEN KIMBERLY. Dr. Frank Winship, a graduate of Albany Medical College (1888), served as Brunswick's health officer for 25 years. It has been said he kept two teams of horses so he would always be prepared to make a house call. In the winter, if the snow was deep, he would sometimes abandon his cutter and walk on snowshoes to reach the patient. Dr. Frank Winship married Nellie McChesney. (Courtesy Elizabeth Winship Nicoll.)

39

THE PRITCHARD HOME, BUILT C. 1840, FORMERLY AT 227 TAMARAC ROAD. This house was believed to have been built by John Pritchard and, in 1843, was acquired by Joel Bornt. Three of Joel's five children were buried in a small cemetery on the property. In the early 1960s, ownership passed to the Yacevich family. The house was intentionally burned in 1973 and a new one erected on its foundation. (Brunswick Historical Society Collection.)

AN ENIGMATIC HOUSE, TAMARAC ROAD. This house was known to have existed on Tamarac Road but its precise location has been a subject of dispute. It serves an excellent example of Federal-period architecture. The wing to the left may have housed a summer kitchen, woodshed, and carriage storage on its lower floor, and quarters for hired help on the second story. A woodpile is ready to be stacked or stored for the family's fuel supply. It appears two or more fireplaces may have provided heat. (Courtesy Phil Pollock.)

Three

REMEMBERING OUR YOUTH

RUTH L. PATRIE (1894–1955) AND HER PET SHEEP, 227 BRUNSWICK ROAD, AUGUST 31, 1902. Ruth's parents were Lawrence A. Patrie and Mary Elizabeth Colehamer. The house where Ruth lived was built *c.* 1811 by her Colehamer ancestors. Ruth married Fred J. Schafer and they had three sons, one of whom yet resides in the Colehamer home. The barn on the left, behind Ruth, once served as a tollgate along the turnpike that became Brunswick Road (Route 2). It had stood on the opposite side of the road and was moved when the tollgate relocated (see p. 15). The barn was taken down in 1933, long after the time Ruth hitched her sheep to the little cart for excursions around the barnyard. Looking at the photograph of a child causes one to ponder the time in which the youngster lived as well as the child's future. (Courtesy Elizabeth Schafer.)

TWINS OLIVE AND ALBERT FILM WITH THEIR PARENTS, SOPHIA HINKEL AND ANSON FILM, c. 1897. The Film twins, born in 1890, are pictured at their home at 245 Pinewoods Avenue. The family moved to 1036 Spring Avenue in 1901 but Albert later operated a slaughterhouse at this Pinewoods Avenue home. Olive, the only girl in a family of seven children, married Leroy Butler in 1917 and had two children. A hand pump to the right of young Albert supplied the family's water. To the right of the house is a wooden barrel, probably used to catch rainwater from a gutter. This water would have been used for laundry or to water the animals. (Courtesy Jeanne Butler Jarrett.)

WILLIAM "BILL" ROWE (1892–1970), POSING WITH HIS BICYCLE AT A PHOTOGRAPHER'S STUDIO. Bill, the son of Henry Rowe Jr. and Jenny Ferguson, grew up in a house on Creek Road. His father operated a foundry along the Poestenkill Creek near Eagle Mills. Bill later operated a slaughterhouse and meat market on the property where he had lived in his youth. He also ran the Old Heidelberg (see p. 90). Bill married Mary Grant and they had two children. (Courtesy Mr. and Mrs. Henry Rowe.)

MILO HYDE SR. AND HIS MOTHER, 1919.
Milo, the son of Nellie and Daniel Hyde, was born at the Roberts Farm off the Town Office Road. Milo served in the U.S. Army during World War II and married Harriet Weatherwax (see p. 61). They had two children (see p. 53). Milo worked for the office of the Rensselaer County Clerk. (Courtesy Milo Hyde Sr.)

MILO HYDE SR. WITH TAMARAC SCHOOLCHILDREN DURING FIRE PREVENTION WEEK, 1963. Troy photographer Harry McKenna produced this picture, which appeared in *The Times Record*, as the Troy newspaper was then known. Milo, chief of the Center Brunswick Volunteer Fire Company, and two colleagues, Carl O'Brien and Harold Dunham (Eagle Mills Volunteer Fire Company), explain how to use a fire extinguisher. All the children have been given helmets as souvenirs. The Taconic-Raymertown Kiwanis cosponsored the event. (Courtesy Center Brunswick Ladies Auxiliary.)

SISTERS MILDRED (RIGHT) AND M. LOUISE MCCHESNEY, DAUGHTERS OF WALTER AND CORINNE MORRISON MCCHESNEY, C. 1915. Descendants of two of Cropseyville's early families, Mildred and Louise enjoyed a rich heritage, much of which Mildred recorded in publications of the Brunswick Historical Society. While working for the New York State Department of Education, Mildred was the first woman named to the position of supervisor of the social studies department. Louise married Alfred L. Coonradt and for many years operated the Amber Lantern Restaurant in Cropseyville. (Courtesy Mildred McChesney.)

LESLIE PHILIP POLLOCK (BORN 1915) AND FRANK ALFRED POLLOCK (1916–1989), TWO OF THE FOUR CHILDREN OF PHILIP P. POLLOCK (SEE P. 117) AND BLANCHE NEWCOMB. These little fellows apparently took great delight in posing for the camera. Leslie later worked in the construction trades as a building inspector and Frank worked as a delivery man and farmer. (Courtesy Phil Pollock.)

JOHN E. LYND (1912–1986), SON OF
JOHN LYND AND ANNA TAMM. John
grew up at the home of his maternal
grandparents, Ernest and Minnie Tamm
(see p. 29), as his mother died when he
was three years old. John worked in the
building trades, repaired antique clocks,
was a member and officer of the Eagle
Mills Volunteer Fire Company, and
enjoyed photography. He married Marion
Keyes and they had two children.
(Courtesy Marion Lynd.)

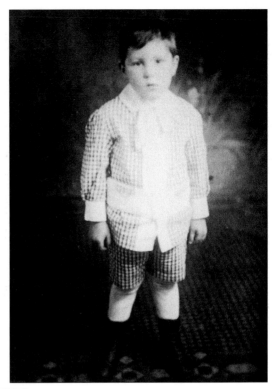

ARNOLD SLITER, SON OF HOWARD AND
ELIZA SLITER. Arnold was born in Troy in
1911 and moved to Eagle Mills when he
was eight years old. He attended the
Garfield School and became acquainted
with John E. Lynd. The two continued
their friendship through life and lived in
nearby residences in Eagle Mills. (Courtesy
Arnold Sliter.)

45

J. Roswell Lee (left) with his parents, Grace Mayer and Joseph G. Lee, 1890s. Dell Hoffay, with horses, posed with the family when this picture was taken. The Lee family lived in the house at 545 Pinewoods Avenue, later owned by Charles Wagar. Roswell's father was a rural mail carrier and farmer. Joseph Lee later moved his family to the VanZandt house (see p. 16) and founded Lee's Dairy, operated by Roswell until the 1960s. He married Florence Carner. (Town of Brunswick Collection.)

Ethel Miller (1897–1996), daughter of Emma Mayer and Elmer Miller, c. 1912. Ethel was Roswell Lee's cousin. She is shown here in her teen years, relaxing in a hammock on the porch of her parents' home on McChesney Avenue Extension at Bonesteel Lane (see p. 125). The barns associated with the Miller Farm stood across the road and are reflected in the window to the right. Ethel, who enjoyed photography, later lived on Maple Avenue in Eagle Mills (see pp. 33 and 118). (Courtesy Irene Miller.)

MARSH E. WAGAR (1911–1988), SON OF FRANCES AND ELMER WAGAR. In this 1925 photograph, Marsh is feeding the chickens on the Keyes Farm. He is in his teen years and is perhaps dressed for school or church. (Courtesy Barbara Hewitt.)

MARSH E. WAGAR BY HIS MEAT DELIVERY TRUCK, 1950S. Marsh started work as a butcher in 1933 and delivered meat to homes in Grafton as well as Brunswick. He also operated a meat market behind his Eagle Mills home on Brunswick Road. (Courtesy Ronald and Helen Wagar.)

THE IVES SISTERS DOING LAUNDRY AT THEIR UNCLE ELMER WHEELER'S FARM ON DATER HILL ROAD, C. 1929. From left to right, Dorothy, Ruth, and Marjorie, daughters of Gladys Cottrell and Alson Ives, try their hands at washing clothes the old-fashioned way. Dorothy later recreated laundry days like the one enjoyed by her and her sisters for the many classes she visited while serving as Brunswick Town Historian (1985–1993). (Courtesy Dorothy Ives McChesney.)

DOROTHY IVES'S WEDDING DAY, CHRISTMAS DAY, 1945. It was during World War II that Dorothy posed with her sisters again for the camera on the occasion of her marriage to Donald E. McChesney, who was then serving with the U.S. Navy. Dorothy's sisters, Ruth Ives (Daley) and Marjorie Ives (Wagar), stand to the groom's right. Also in the wedding party were Mrs. Edwin R. Cottrell, Audrey C. Schmay, Kathryn J. Cottrell, William W. Sharpe, Joseph H. Cottrell, David F. Boyd, Maynard C. Jones, and Arthur S. Jones. The flower girl was Carol Holland and the ring bearer was David E. Wagar. (Courtesy Dorothy Ives McChesney.)

48

DONALD W. CLICKNER (RIGHT) AND HIS GRANDFATHER, WEBSTER M. CLICKNER, C. 1920. Webster M. Clickner served as a justice of the peace (1912–1915) and as town supervisor (1916–1919), but it was his Alaskan adventures that made the local press. In 1898, Webster joined a group of local men traveling to Alaska in search of gold. Many years later, Donald also traveled to Alaska and retraced his grandfather's steps. He later published an account of both his and Webster's Alaskan journeys in the book *Golden Nuggets About Alaska*. Donald Clickner, a machinist by trade, is a well-known authority on antique engines. The son of Sylvia French and Wesley Clickner, Donald has lived in Eagle Mills most of his life and is married to Helen Pollock. (Courtesy Donald W. Clickner.)

ALFRED F. POLLOCK (RIGHT) AND HIS COUSIN, JESSE GARDNER (SEATED FRONT), AT A BEACH ON LONG ISLAND, NEW YORK, C. 1921. Alfred F. Pollock was the uncle of the boys pictured on p. 44 and grew up on the farm of his father, Franklin Pierce Pollock. In this scene, Alfred is high-school age. Jesse Gardner was the son of Bertha Carner Gardner, who relocated from Brunswick to Long Island, where she managed a weekly newspaper, *The Sag Harbor Express*. These lads are wearing bathing suits made of wool. (Courtesy Phil Pollock.)

E. JOAN FARRELL, C. 1930. Joan, the daughter of Esther McKeon and William Farrell, poses with the bridal party's bouquets on the lawn of the McKeon home on the wedding day of her Aunt Eleanor McKeon. Miss Farrell later pursued a teaching career and was associated with the Averill Park school system. (Courtesy E. Joan Farrell.)

KATHERINE LANSING FILM (1887–1941). Katherine was the daughter of Elizabeth Pfeil and George Lansing and married Anson Film Jr. (1884–1946), a cattle dealer who was a brother to the Film twins pictured on p. 65. Katherine had three children, Kenneth Lansing, Doris Elizabeth, and Donald George. This photograph of Katherine, probably taken before she was married, was treasured by her son Donald and depicts the photographer's skill in presenting an attractive woman to her best advantage. (Courtesy Carolyn Film.)

KENNETH L. FILM (1919–1977) AND HIS SISTER, DORIS ELIZABETH FILM (BORN 1922), TWO OF THE THREE CHILDREN OF KATHERINE LANSING AND ANSON FILM JR., C. 1926. The Film family resided in Center Brunswick. Kenneth and his brother Donald operated the Trojan Frozen Food Locker on Hoosick Road for several years and later moved to Maryland, where he became an interior decorator. Doris married Bernard Scanlon and relocated to Florida. (Courtesy Carolyn Film.)

CAROLYN FILM (EDWARDS) AND HER SISTER, FRANCES FILM (FELLNER), WITH TONY THE PONY, C. 1928. These girls, the daughters of Olive St. John (see pp. 34 and 100) and Walter Film, lived in Center Brunswick and attended the McKinley School. Carolyn later recalled that a photographer with a pony sometimes visited the school and took the children's pictures. Posing a child astride a pony for photographing was popular during the 1920s and 1930s. (Courtesy Carolyn Film Edwards.)

ELEANOR LEE (HILL), DAUGHTER OF ELSA SNYDER AND MERRILL T. LEE, C. 1940. Eleanor Lee, now the wife of Anthony Hill, is seen practicing her accordion, but she later pursued a career in nursing, not music. Eleanor cherishes this photograph because the home in the background held so many memories of people special to her. It was the home of Frank and Ella Smith and, later, a convalescent home operated by Chester and Nina Wyman. The house stood on Hoosick Road and was razed in 1997. (Courtesy Eleanor Lee Hill.)

HARRY McISAAC TEST DRIVING A CAR MADE BY NEIGHBOR LOUIS MILLER, 1954. Harry McIsaac, son of George and Harriet McIsaac, grew up in Center Brunswick where he spent much time visiting his neighbor, Louis Miller (see p. 106). Mr. Miller made these kiddie cars more for fun than profit. Harry continues to make his home in Brunswick and is engaged in the building trades. (From the album of the late Veronica Miller.)

MILO "BUTCH" HYDE JR. AND HIS SISTER, SANDI HYDE (LAVIOLETTE), CHILDREN OF MILO HYDE SR. AND HARRIET WEATHERWAX, SHOWING OFF THEIR CHRISTMAS GIFTS, 1954. By the 1950s, every home in Brunswick probably had a television set but Christmas morning was too busy a time for watching. Butch is ready to take on the bad guys with his new toy guns while Sandi models a drum majorette's uniform. Butch, the father of two daughters, later served in the U.S. Air Force during the Vietnam War and chose a career in sales. Sandi is the mother of two children and has served as Brunswick Town Clerk. (Courtesy Milo Hyde Sr.)

THE FREDDIE FREIHOFER TELEVISION SHOW, 1962. Charles Freihofer, owner of a Philadelphia bakery, established the Freihofer Bakery in Lansingburgh in 1913 and soon introduced the home delivery of baked goods by horse-drawn vehicles. About the time the horse-drawn delivery wagons were retired, the Freddie Freihofer Show appeared on television. Local youngsters celebrating a birthday were invited to appear as participants. Erin Boylan (Hoernig) of Eagle Mills, pictured fourth from the right in the second row, was one of several local youngsters who made their television debut with Freddie. Erin later served in the U.S. Navy; she relocated to Virginia, married, and has two sons. (Courtesy Mary B. Knox.)

KELLY ANN QUIGLEY, A CEREBRAL PALSY TELETHON THEME CHILD, 1970. Kelly, who resided near the hamlet of Tamarac, was five years old when chosen to appear on the televised telethon carried on WTEN-TV. Kelly now lives in a nearby town, is married, and has three children. This photograph appeared in *The Times Record*. (Town of Brunswick Collection.)

Four

BONDS OF COMMUNITY

THE ENSIGN POST BAND, 1889. The Ensign Post was the local chapter of the GAR (Grand Army of the Republic) and it sponsored this band. The band marched in parades and performed at various community celebrations. The members of the band were volunteers who believed in the principles of the organization, enjoyed the camaraderie realized through participation, and appreciated the recognition given them by the local community. The ever-changing needs of people and of the community have encouraged the formation of various groups and organizations at different times in our history, enriching the lives of their members while strengthening the bonds of community. (Brunswick Historical Society Collection.)

A QUILTING PARTY, 1896. Andrew Mullin (see p. 98) may have photographed this group of Brunswickers who traveled to the nearby town of Grafton for a quilting party. The group was probably having a good time until the camera appeared and everyone had to "hold still." From left to right they are as follows: (front row) Bertha Whyland Clum, Florence Mullin (Reed), Edward Coons, Lulu Stewart, and Elleda Wagar Tamm; (second row) Sarah Allen, Amanda Stewart, and Martha Coonrad; (back row) Etta and Dexter Coons, Sarah Mullin, Bertha Coonrad Ferguson, Charles Coonrad, and Frank Ferguson. (Town of Brunswick Collection.)

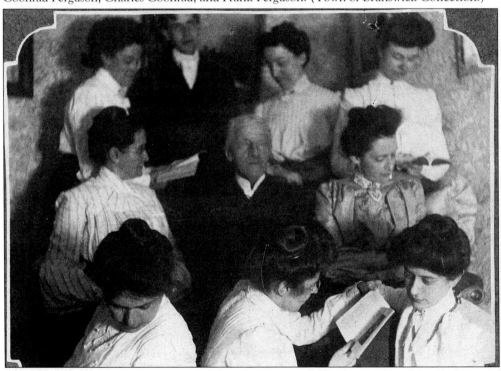

THE SHAKESPEARE CLUB, C. 1902. Neither the origins nor the conclusion of the Shakespeare Club are known but it apparently encouraged the dramatic interests of a number of Cropseyville women. Clockwise from the back row are Billy Kilmer, Belle Hoffman, Nellie Green, Carrie McChesney, Carrie Green, Clara Hulbert, Louise Newbury, Mrs. Albert Green, Mary Gibson, and Rev. C.H. Kilmer, who was the minister at the First Presbyterian Church of Brunswick and, possibly, the group's advisor. (Courtesy Mildred McChesney.)

THE YELLOW DOG CLUB, OR, THE ORDER OF UNITED AMERICAN MECHANICS (OUAM), c. 1900. This group has been identified as the Order of United American Mechanics that met in Center Brunswick beginning in the late 19th century. The photograph's owner said his father called this the Yellow Dog Club. Note the statue of a dog on the stool in front of the group. The OUAM was a fraternal order of men who worked in mechanical occupations. Yellow dog contracts were agreements made between employers and non-union workers hired during a strike that they would not affiliate with a union. Old photographs are often unwilling to share their secrets. (Courtesy Ray Shaver.)

A c. 1910 INDEPENDENCE DAY PARADE, EAGLE MILLS. The Fourth of July was celebrated with a parade in many hamlets. The porch of the Eagle Mills Hotel is lined with spectators (see p. 21). After the parade, families and friends continued the day's celebration with a picnic lunch that probably included homemade ice cream. It was a day for fun and relaxation just as it is today. (Brunswick Historical Society Collection.)

THE INDEPENDENT ORDER OF ODD FELLOWS (IOOF), LODGE NO. 711, CROPSEYVILLE, c. 1949. Jack Short, a talented Troy photographer whose work appeared in local newspapers, photographed the IOOF on the occasion of an installation of officers. Pictured are, from left to right, as follows: (front row) Henry Fitting, Fred Reiner, Al Shaver, and James Spiak Sr.; (back row) Charles Vogt, Carl Boomhower, Art Jones, Les Haynor, and Darwin Miller. The IOOF existed for more than 75 years. About 1993, the few remaining members of the group sold their Cropseyville lodge to an auctioneer. (Courtesy Leonard Roden.)

BRUNSWICK GRANGE NO. 1337, 40TH ANNIVERSARY, 1954. The Grange was formed in 1867 to improve the economic conditions of farmers by influencing government policy and legislation. The National Grange issued a charter to the Brunswick Grange on July 1, 1914. The Brunswick Grange has offered the community educational programs, entertainment, and dinners over the years. Cutting the organization's anniversary cake, from left to right, are Don Bonesteel, Harold Goyer, Flora Bonesteel, and Edith Haynor. The Brunswick Grange is the town's longest-surviving community organization. (Courtesy Brunswick Grange.)

A Brunswick Presbyterian Church play program, 1939. Churches and other organizations often sponsored plays and concerts, sometimes to raise funds, but mostly to encourage fellowship among members and provide the community wholesome entertainment. Note the church included a little jingle on the program identifying its service area. Today, this church has a great many members from beyond the local community. (Courtesy Mildred McChesney.)

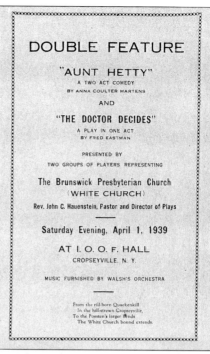

DOUBLE FEATURE

"AUNT HETTY"
A TWO ACT COMEDY
BY ANNA COULTER MARTENS

AND

"THE DOCTOR DECIDES"
A PLAY IN ONE ACT
BY FRED EASTMAN

PRESENTED BY
TWO GROUPS OF PLAYERS REPRESENTING

The Brunswick Presbyterian Church
(WHITE CHURCH)
Rev. John C. Hauenstein, Pastor and Director of Plays

Saturday Evening, April 1, 1939

AT I. O. O. F. HALL
CROPSEYVILLE, N. Y.

MUSIC FURNISHED BY WALSH'S ORCHESTRA

From the rill-born Quackenkill
In the hill-strewn Cropseyville,
To the Poesten's larger lands
The White Church bound extends.

A Lenten play, *The Symbol of the Cross*, Eagle Mills Methodist Church, 1958. This performance, complete with appropriate costumes, was well rehearsed by the young members of the cast that included the following, from left to right: (front row) Allen Waterfield, Bette Ann Weeden, and Ruth Lynd; (back row) Judy Boomhower, Robert Blocksidge, Chester Winsor, Kenneth Herrington, and Terry Perkins. (Courtesy Hope United Methodist Church.)

THE EAGLE MILLS VOLUNTEER FIRE DEPARTMENT WITH THE FIRST PUMPER, C. 1929.
Brunswick's first fire department was in Eagle Mills and its first chief was John Hook. In 1929, the Rensselaer County Board of Supervisors, predecessor to the current county legislature, granted the Town of Brunswick approval to establish Eagle Mills Fire District No. 1. The district's first motorized apparatus was the 1929 American LaFrance GMC engine pictured here at the intersection of Brunswick and Creek Roads. The World War I monument, erected in 1919, is seen to the right. (Brunswick Historical Society Collection.)

THE EAGLE MILLS FIREHOUSE, BUILT 1947, BRUNSWICK ROAD (ROUTE 2), EAGLE MILLS, PHOTOGRAPHED 1971. The Eagle Mills Fire Department garaged its equipment at John Dixon's store and Harold Winne's creamery before the firehouse was built to the west of the old Eagle Mills Hotel. An addition was added in 1957 following the formation of a rescue squad and purchase of an ambulance. In 1979, a new firehouse was built at 627 Brunswick Road. The old firehouse is privately owned today. (Courtesy Harold Dunham.)

THE CENTER BRUNSWICK VOLUNTEER FIRE COMPANY, 1951. The Center Brunswick Volunteer Fire Company was incorporated in 1945 and its first firehouse was built in 1946. A new firehouse was built in 1989 on an adjacent site. The firemen shown here are, from left to right, as follows: (front row) Hiram Sheffer, Bill Dougherty, Leroy Banker, Kenneth Stannard, Bernard Carroll Jr., Ralph Shaffer, Carl O'Brien (chief), Paul Mandeville, Robert Mandeville, William Goyer, William Carroll, Robert Goyer, and Thomas Carroll; (back row) Kenneth Lawton, Freeman Bonesteel, Ralph Grandjean, Edward Heidelmark, Carl Bulson, Eugene Hunter, Joseph Goewey, Charles McCreedy, Ray Bonesteel, Milo Hyde, James Gemmill Jr., Edward Sullivan, Howard Wagar, and Robert Hyde Jr. (Courtesy Milo Hyde.)

THE CENTER BRUNSWICK FIRE COMPANY LADIES AUXILIARY DURING A CHRISTMAS PARTY AT THE CENTER BRUNSWICK METHODIST CHURCH, 1956. The ladies serving Carl O'Brien his meal are, from left to right, Marge Potts, Peggy Carroll, Harriet Hyde, Loretta Goyer, and Helen Campbell. This was a "dime-a-dip" supper; each helping of food cost 10¢. The Ladies Auxiliary was formed in 1947. (Courtesy Center Brunswick Ladies Auxiliary.)

THE MOUNTAIN VIEW VOLUNTEER FIRE COMPANY, 1947. The Mountain View Volunteer Fire Company was formed in 1944 by those who had participated in the civilian defense units that served the Mountain View neighborhood during World War II. The first chief was Willard Simpson. The company's firehouse was built in 1947 on the site of the Mountain View Community Center (see p. 14). The company has since expanded its facility. (Courtesy Mountain View Volunteer Fire Company.)

A MOUNTAIN VIEW FIRE COMPANY'S LADIES AUXILIARY CLAMSTEAM, JULY 31, 1949. The Mountain View Fire Company's Ladies Auxiliary was formed in 1944 and its first president was Ruth Prefontaine. The ladies taking a break from their kitchen duties are, from left to right, as follows: (front) Mary Manning; (middle row) Ruth Prefontaine, Marge Riley, Marge Lawless, and Della Gauthier; (back row) Ethel Kline, Mamie Riordan, and Albena Alarie. (Courtesy Mountain View Ladies Auxiliary.)

BRUNSWICK VOLUNTEER FIRE COMPANY NO. 1, FOUNDED IN 1943 AND ORGANIZED IN 1944. The early members of Brunswick No. 1 built their first truck (shown here), using an Army surplus trailer pump and a 1938 Dodge chassis, for about $1,000. It has been said the firemen sometimes had to push the truck to get it running! The truck was kept in Archie Jones's garage at 566 Hoosick Street until the company built its firehouse on land donated by Mr. Jones. The company moved to a new firehouse in 1992. (Courtesy Brunswick No. 1 Volunteer Fire Company.)

A FIREMEN'S DINNER, C. 1960. Among this group of area firemen were two prominent Brunswick fire chiefs, John J. "Jack" Leary (third from left) and Maynard Dixon (third from right). Jack Leary was a founder of the Brunswick No. 1 Volunteer Fire Company and its first chief. He was also the first Rensselaer County Fire Coordinator. Maynard Dixon, also Brunswick Town Supervisor (1960–1966), was chief of the Eagle Mills Volunteer Fire Company from 1948 to 1962 and president of the Rensselaer County Fire Chief's Association. Both men were honored, on separate occasions, for their extraordinary dedication and many contributions. (Courtesy Brunswick No. 1 Volunteer Fire Company.)

SPEIGELTOWN VOLUNTEER FIRE COMPANY CHARTER MEMBERS, 1945. Speigeltown, in the town of Schagticoke, is northwest of Brunswick. In 1949, the Speigeltown Volunteers agreed to provide fire protection to the northwestern part of Brunswick. The company was granted its charter in 1944. This photograph was taken at a clamsteam at Miami Beach. The group includes, from left to right, the following: (front row) Irv Gordon, Kenneth Lape, James McNary, William Perkins, Walter Wood, and Joseph Rodriquez; (back row) Edward Palmer, Harold Damon, John Murphy, Irving Dutcher, Tony Hansen, Neil Kelleher, John Knauer, and Frank Langen. (Courtesy Al Damon.)

THE BRUNSWICK SPORTSMAN'S CLUB, C. 1940. The Brunswick Sportsman's Club was formed in 1938 and soon acquired an 85-acre farm near Cropseyville for its clubhouse and target practice ranges. Pictured here are some of the club's early members in their clubhouse. From left to right they are as follows: (front row) Myron Charenger, Ruby Charenger, Jesse O'Donnell, Edna Rifenburg, Dick Robb, Ruth Rifenburg, Marion Hakes, Margaret McLoughlin, unidentified, and Bill McLoughlin; (back row) Leslie Hakes, ? Rossetti, Hap Coonrad, Phil Davis, unidentified, Earl Rifenburg, unidentified, ? Whipple, Fred Abduhl, Hap Snyder, and Jack Abduhl. (Courtesy Ceil Boomhower.)

A Mountain View Home Bureau hayride at Sam and Mabel Miller's farm, April 7, 1949. Fifty years ago several home-bureau units existed in Brunswick. The organization offered lessons in cooking, food preservation, child care, sewing, and crafts. Meetings were generally held at members' homes. Sam and Mabel Miller's son Warren is driving the tractor. The lady waving at the camera is Albena Alarie, who also appears on pp. 62 and 104. (Courtesy Iva Riordan.)

The Trojan Frozen Food Locker Bowling League, 1953–54. Bowling became very popular following World War II and many local businesses sponsored leagues to promote good will. The Trojan Frozen Food Locker was operated by Donald and Kenneth Film (see p. 51) on the Hoosick Road. The plaque indicates the business's location as Troy because Brunswick mail is handled by the Troy postal service. (Brunswick Historical Society Collection.)

BRUNSWICK SCOUT TROOP #27, CAMP ROTARY, DAVITT'S LAKE, POESTENKILL, 1952.
Camp Rotary was presented as a gift to all Boy Scouts in Rensselaer County by the Troy Rotary Club in 1923. Enjoying this outing are, from left to right, Richard Gilbert, Ronald Sanders, Gene Boomhower, and Robert Dayton. (Courtesy Ceil Boomhower.)

CAMP FIRE GIRLS, 1970. This Camp Fire group created its name, Cidoroga Checalysu, using syllables from each member's name. The girls are wearing wing dresses they made following the study of a West Coast Native-American tribe. Under the guidance of Dorothy Ives McChesney (see p. 48), who served with the Camp Fire Council many years, area girls studied Native-American cultures, nature, and crafts. (Courtesy Dorothy Ives McChesney.)

THE C. 1909 EAGLE MILLS BASEBALL TEAM. Earlier in this century, each community supported an adult baseball team at one time or another. This team included, from left to right, the following members: (front row) Clifford Hayner, Edward Gardner, unidentified, Joel Holcomb, Walter Weigner, and Ernest Tamm; (back row) Orrie Austin, John Lynd (umpire), Adam Crystal, Stanton Edwards, and Peter Darby. In the front is mascot William J. Tamm. Mr. Holcomb, who lost an arm in an industrial accident at the Planter's Hoe Company, amazed everyone when he batted with his right arm alone. Holcomb served as Brunswick Town Clerk from 1934 to 1941. (Courtesy Marion Lynd.)

THE GREEN HORNETS BASEBALL TEAM, BRUNSWICK LITTLE LEAGUE, 1965. Brunswick Little League has served young ball players for more than 40 years. This team included the following, from left to right: (front row) unidentified, Doug Pouie, Dennis Ned, three unidentified, Mario Rindone, Brian Denue, and unidentified; (back row) Mr. Gould, Tracy Carnivale, Paul Snyder, Patrick Poleto, Tim Gallagher, Kevin Gould, Tom Thomas, Jim Keith, and unidentified. Several of the individuals pictured now watch their sons play in the Brunswick Little League. (Photograph by Bill DeFilippis; courtesy Patrick Poleto.)

THE TACONIC-RAYMERTOWN KIWANIS, 1971. This group was formed in the 1960s. In 1971 each Kiwanis chapter in the nation was asked to undertake a project involving "one clean mile of country road." The local chapter chose to clean up Route 278 and restore the Clum's Corners District No. 6 School (see p. 72). Pictured are, from left to right, William Engelke, New York State Assemblyman Neil Kelleher, Rev. Peter Swarez (who was associated with the Gilead Lutheran Church), Bob Campana, Marsh Miron, and Joe Reneud. (Courtesy William Engelke.)

A PARADE FLOAT IN THE TOWN OF BRUNSWICK'S 175TH ANNIVERSARY CELEBRATION, 1982. Kenneth Clickner (left) and Harold Ives reenacted a scene representing the time in our history when much of Rensselaer County was subject to ground rents payable on the first day of every year to the Van Rensselear Family. The rents were payable in the form of bushels of "marketable winter wheat, fat fowl, and service with a team and wagon." It was not until after the "anti-rent period" (c. 1839–1860), a time of resistance marked by warfare and political maneuvering, that landholders were able to obtain clear titles to their land. This photograph by Tom Killips appeared June 6, 1982, in *The Sunday Record*. (Courtesy Mr. and Mrs. Donald W. Clickner.)

Five

SCHOOL DAYS

SCHOOL DISTRICT NO. 2, THE GARFIELD SCHOOL, EAGLE MILLS, 1891. The photographer made great efforts to ensure each student in this large class would be clearly visible in the finished image. Pictured from left to right are the following: (front row) unidentified, James Rourke, William Malone, three unidentified, Stella Rourke, Minnie Marshall, Ina Fritz, two unidentified, Robert Folderman, and Sherman Folderman; (second row) teacher Charles Hawley, ? Ryan, Stella Steinberg, Nellie Link, Edna VanZandt, Elleda Wagar, Nellie Shyne, Hattie McChesney, Eliza Wagar, Cora Mambert, Grace Mayer, Mabel Coonrad, and teacher Mayme Hydorn; (third row) ? Ryan, two unidentified, Addie Butler, unidentified, Kate Ryan, Bessie Bulson, unidentified, Fred Rohrwasser, Arthur Fritz, Leddra Wagar, and Cora Mayer; (back row) Francis St. Laurent, Clarence St. Laurent, Stanley Colehamer, Hiram Ryan, Frank Jones, Wilson Wagar, unidentified, Harry Rowe, and three unidentified. Interestingly, everyone in the photograph is wearing a hat. Grades one through four were assigned one teacher, and grades five through eight the other. Several of the individuals pictured here held a class reunion at the Amber Lantern Restaurant in Cropseyville in 1966. (Town of Brunswick Collection.)

SCHOOL DISTRICT NO. 1, THE GEORGE WASHINGTON SCHOOL, MENEMSHA LANE AT LANSING ROAD, 1896. It seems the entire population of the district, also known as the Springer District, turned out to be photographed. The George Washington School was built in 1885. Two brick additions of a modern design, rectangular and utilitarian, were later added to the old schoolhouse. In 1970, the old schoolhouse burned. Operated as one of New York's last common school districts, the George Washington School merged with the Averill Park district in 1996. (Town of Brunswick Collection.)

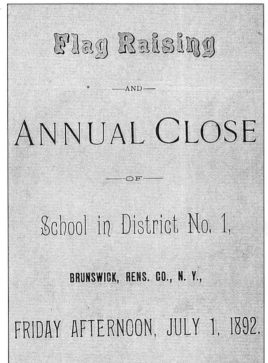

A CLOSE OF SCHOOL PROGRAM OF THE GEORGE WASHINGTON SCHOOL, 1892. This celebration consisted of recitations, dialogues, songs, and instrumental selections. Short speeches by area clergy and music by the East Brunswick Band rounded out the day's event. Sixty-eight students attended this school in 1892. (Town of Brunswick Collection.)

School District No. 5, the McKinley School, 1011 Hoosick Road (Route 7). The two-room McKinley School was built about 1872; it is probable an earlier school occupied the same site. This school served briefly as a youth center in the early 1970s. Next it was acquired by one of its former students, who operated a printing business here. The school now serves an office of a local attorney. (Town of Brunswick Collection.)

School District No. 5, a McKinley School class, 1909. The students in attendance when this image was created included the following, from left to right: (front row) Mildred Hayner, Earl Sheffer, Clara Gummer, Herbie Vroman, and Chesta Smith; (second row) George Gummer, Marion File, primary teacher Jennie Cushman, principal Clara Marcellus, Martha Whitmore, Gladys Zion, Marion Baud, and Florence Miltz; (third row) Allen Hayner, George Wachtel, Walter Film, Clara Miltz, Wilda Williams, Blanche Vroman, Margaret Sheffer, Eleanor Wachtel, and Henrietta Clum; (back row) Eugene Hunter, Lester Freemantle, George Marcelles, Elmer Goard, Ralph Sheffer, Willard Abbott, Walter Derrick, Charles Vroman, and (by the window) Irving Derrick. (Town of Brunswick Collection.)

SCHOOL DISTRICT NO. 6, THE LINCOLN SCHOOL, BUILT C. 1830, ROUTE 278 AT CLUM'S CORNERS. Known also as the Rocky Road School and Little Red Schoolhouse, this is Brunswick's oldest surviving schoolhouse and it is owned by the Brittonkill School District. Seen in this undated image is teacher Minnie Esther Davis. This school last operated as a district school in 1952 and was briefly reopened by the Brittonkill District about 1958. In the 1970s the building was restored by the Taconic-Raymertown Kiwanis. (Brunswick Historical Society Collection.)

ARBOR DAY, THE DISTRICT NO. 6 SCHOOL. Teacher Florence Bulson Hayner's 1930 class celebrated Arbor Day by cleaning up the school grounds. Shown here are the following, from left to right: (front row) Mildred Eddy, Louise Eddy, Pearl Shaver, four unidentified, Ray Trzcinski, Evelyn Hoffman, and Wilbur Hoffman; (back row) Mary Land Bornt, Vivian Shaver, Clarence Newton, Kenneth Wagar, Ira Bulson, Harold Folsbee, Paul Bulson, Donald Shaver and Carl Shaver. (Courtesy Clarence Newton.)

THE PLEASANT VALLEY SCHOOL AND THE EAST BRUNSWICK METHODIST CHURCH, C. 1912, ROUTE 2, CROPSEYVILLE. The East Brunswick Methodist Church was formed in 1874 and disbanded about 1938; the church structure was sold to the Boomhower family and converted to a residence. The Pleasant Valley School was built in 1889 by Josiah McChesney and replaced two smaller schools, one on South Road and one east of this site known as the Rock Hollow School. Aaron Davis was the trustee and Maggie Delo the first teacher. The schoolhouse today is also used as a residence. (Courtesy Mildred McChesney.)

THE INTERIOR OF THE PLEASANT VALLEY SCHOOL, C. 1899. An old newspaper account describes the features of this classroom on its opening day as a single room with a Carolina pine ceiling, black walnut trimmings, and floors of yellow pine. The room was originally furnished with 55 desks, a teacher's desk, and two recitation settees. About 1915, the single classroom was divided into two classrooms. (Brunswick Historical Society Collection.)

73

SCHOOL DISTRICT NO. 7, THE VANARNUM SCHOOL, GRANGE ROAD (ROUTE 142). The brick District No. 7 school was built to replace an earlier frame structure that stood on Gypsy Lane. The earlier school was once the classroom of Herman Melville, who resided in Lansingburgh and worked as a teacher. In 1953, the brick schoolhouse and one-half acre of land were offered for sale at public auction; the structure was converted to a residence. Children residing in this district were transferred to the Lansingburgh School. (Brunswick Historical Society Collection.)

THE TAMARAC SCHOOL, DISTRICT NO. 12, CAMEL HILL ROAD, BUILT 1864, NOW DESTROYED. The Tamarac School had its own well and pump for water in its front yard, but not many windows. Poestenkill Town Historian Florence Hill taught in this school early in her teaching career. The building collapsed from the weight of snow during the winter of 1994–95. (Town of Brunswick Collection.)

TEACHER M. LOUISE NEWBURY,
c. 1910. Miss Newbury taught in the
Cropseyville area for about 50 years; her
assignments included the Clum's
Corners School, the White Church
School, and the Pleasant Valley School.
About 1910, this popular teacher
presented her students this holiday
souvenir with her photograph. On
another occasion, she gave her students
copies of a class picture from which she
had deliberately cut her own image!
(Courtesy Mildred McChesney.)

TEACHER OLIVE RODEN LYND AND HER
HUSBAND, WILLARD. Born in Brunswick,
Olive completed eighth grade in 1910 and
attended high school in Troy. Upon
receipt of her permanent teacher's
certificate, Olive was advised by the
Brunswick School Superintendent to
teach one year out of town. Olive soon
returned to Brunswick to teach at the
Garfield and White Church Schools. Her
teaching career spanned almost 50 years.
She once said Miss Newbury had been her
favorite teacher. (Courtesy Marion Lynd.)

SCHOOL DISTRICT NO. 9, THE MOODY SCHOOL, DATER HILL ROAD, C. 1918. Located southeast of Eagle Mills, this school also served a part of the nearby town of Poestenkill. The little schoolhouse has been converted to a residence. (Courtesy Mr. and Mrs. Donald Clickner.)

A MOODY SCHOOL PICNIC, EARLY 1900S. It is not known whether teacher Esther Pollock Retallick caught any fish on the day she took her Moody School class on an outing to a local pond. In the era of one-room rural schoolhouses, teachers relied on the great outdoors as a scientific laboratory and the likely destination for a class trip. (Courtesy Mr. and Mrs. Donald Clickner.)

A SCHOOL PICNIC PROGRAM AT HAYNERVILLE, SPONSORED BY FREAR'S TROY BAZAAR, 1888. Haynersville was originally spelled without the -s, a tradition that continued through the mid-20th century. This program included several recitations such as "The Little Boy's Lament" by Herbert Hayner, songs, and the five-act comedy *Punkin Ridge*. William H. Frear, a successful Troy merchant, apparently appreciated his Brunswick patrons. It is also interesting the school picnic was held during the summer recess. (Town of Brunswick Collection.)

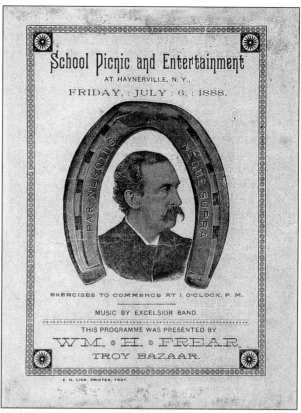

SCHOOL DISTRICT NO. 8, A CLASS OF THE HAYNERSVILLE SCHOOL, C. 1952. The schoolhouse visible behind the students replaced an earlier school that was destroyed by arson in 1924 and has been converted to a residence. Several of the children appear to be very young and may be siblings of some of the students. (Courtesy John and Joann Tarbox.)

SYCAWAY SCHOOL, BRUNSWICK.

THE ARCHITECTURAL DESIGN OF THE SCHOOL DISTRICT NO. 11 SCHOOL, THE SYCAWAY SCHOOL. The Sycaway neighborhood straddles the Troy-Brunswick line and the Sycaway School District was originally a Brunswick school district. This school was built to replace one that stood near the present Lady of Victory Clubhouse. The pictured structure was demolished in 1927 following completion of a brick building at 412 Hoosick Street known as School No. 18. The Sycaway School District remained an independent district, contracting with the Troy school system for services, until mandated by the New York State Education Department to join the Troy School District in 1969. (Town of Brunswick Collection.)

SCHOOL DISTRICT NO. 5, THE LEE SCHOOL, KEYES LANE. Teachers Beulah Brown (second from right) and Mabel Keyes (far right) welcome students to their new school in 1953. Merrill T. Lee (left) oversaw the construction of the school, contributing much of his labor. The school was called the Lee School in recognition of Merrill's leadership and contributions. This school was subsequently conveyed to the Center Brunswick Volunteer Fire Company for use as a social hall after the school closed. It was razed in 1997 for the construction of the Brunswick Community Center. (Courtesy Eleanor Lee Hill.)

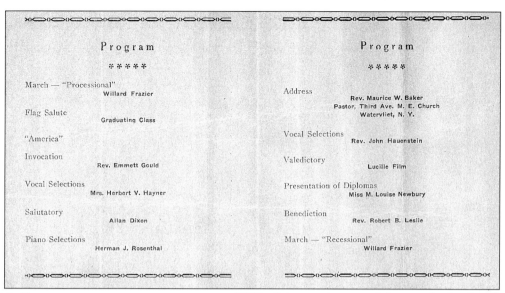

Program

❈ ❈ ❈ ❈ ❈

March — "Processional"
Willard Frazier

Flag Salute
Graduating Class

"America"

Invocation
Rev. Emmett Gould

Vocal Selections
Mrs. Herbert V. Hayner

Salutatory
Allan Dixon

Piano Selections
Herman J. Rosenthal

Program

❈ ❈ ❈ ❈ ❈

Address
Rev. Maurice W. Baker
Pastor, Third Ave. M. E. Church
Watervliet, N. Y.

Vocal Selections
Rev. John Hauenstein

Valedictory
Lucille Film

Presentation of Diplomas
Miss M. Louise Newbury

Benediction
Rev. Robert B. Leslie

March — "Recessional"
Willard Frazier

A BRUNSWICK GRADUATION PROGRAM, 1937. Prior to the consolidation of schools, all Brunswick schools participated in a shared graduation ceremony held at one of the area churches. This program describes the eighth-grade graduation exercises held that year at the Gilead Lutheran Church. (Town of Brunswick Collection.)

THE 1937 BRUNSWICK SCHOOLS GRADUATION, GILEAD LUTHERAN CHURCH. This photograph was produced by the Cassel Studio in Berlin, New York. The students are graduating from the eighth grade. The group includes, from left to right, the following: (front row) Barbara Kline, Mary Costello, Allen Dixon, Lucille Film, and John Dugan; (second row) Raymond Calhoun, Joseph Welch, Marjorie Weidenbacker, Lenore Peckham, Margaret Johnston, and William Miller; (third row) Joe Welch, two unidentified, Henry Trzcinski, and unidentified; (back row) Warren Rymiller, unidentified, Joseph Hedrick, Warren Christian, and William Meyer. (Brunswick Historical Society Collection.)

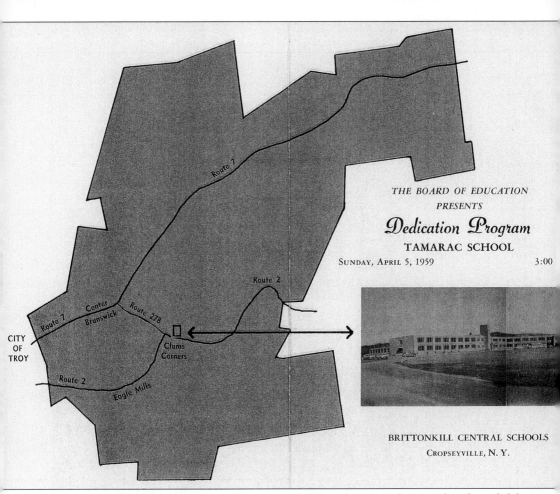

THE BOARD OF EDUCATION
PRESENTS

Dedication Program

TAMARAC SCHOOL

SUNDAY, APRIL 5, 1959   3:00

BRITTONKILL CENTRAL SCHOOLS
CROPSEYVILLE, N. Y.

A TAMARAC SCHOOL DEDICATION PROGRAM, 1959. After several years of study and debate, the centralized Brittonkill School District was formed in 1956 and included parts of Brunswick, Poestenkill, Grafton, and Pittstown. A new educational facility was built east of Clum's Corners. The name of the new school was selected through a student essay contest won by Charles Meeson, who suggested Tamarac. The new district took the name Brittonkill, created using parts of the names of the towns that would send their youth to the new school: *Br* from Brunswick, *-itt* from Pittstown, *-on* from Grafton, and *-kill* from Poestenkill. (Town of Brunswick Collection.)

Six

AROUND THE TOWN

THE BRUNSWICK HIGHWAY GARAGE AND TOWN OFFICES, 308 TOWN OFFICE ROAD, 1963.
This building was built in 1946 by William J. Tamm of Eagle Mills to replace the highway
garage that burned in February 1946. Although this building included space for the town clerk,
meetings of the town's officials continued to be conducted at the town clerk's residence for
several years, a practice that had begun about 1900. Pictured here are Highway Superintendent
A. Frank Bentley (left) and Town Supervisor Maynard Dixon (see p. 63). Bentley served as
highway superintendent from 1962 to 1971 and was the last to obtain this office by election; the
job has since been filled by appointment. The highlight of Dixon's tenure as supervisor occurred
in 1965, when Brunswick's population reached 10,000 and the town was declared a "suburban
town of the first class." (Town of Brunswick Collection.)

THE BRUNSWICK TELEPHONE OFFICE, HOOSICK ROAD (ROUTE 7), CENTER BRUNSWICK, c. 1940. In 1890 the Town of Brunswick gave American Telephone and Telegraph approval to install lines and poles through Center Brunswick. In 1909, the New York Commercial Telephone Company reported the installation of 30 telephones in Brunswick. The Brunswick Telephone Office occupied the right side of this building, owned by Art Derrick, who lived in the other side and ran a greenhouse "out in back." The building was torn down after the telephone exchange was no longer needed. (Courtesy Edith Fichtner.)

BRUNSWICK TELEPHONE OPERATORS, c. 1947. The Brunswick Telephone Office provided dozens of local women employment over its many years of operation. From left to right are Mabel Hunter, Marjorie Carroll O'Brien, and Elsa Lee. It has been said two of the most frequent inquiries to the telephone operators were, "Where's the fire?" and "What time is it?" (Courtesy Eleanor Lee Hill.)

BETTS' CIDER MILL AND HOME, BETWEEN SPRING AVENUE AND PLEASANT VIEW DRIVE. The best known of several Brunswick cider mills was this one, operated by Irving Betts, who started the business at the age of 14! Mr. Betts and his wife, Flora Lape, always had a free apple or cup of cider for the children who stopped by on their way home from the nearby George Washington School. The cider mill burned in 1945, bringing a sad end to what had become a local landmark. (Brunswick Historical Society Collection.)

SHIPPEY'S SNACK BAR, BRUNSWICK ROAD AT SHIPPEY LANE, C. 1930. Jennie Rankin Shippey (second from right) and her husband, William Shippey (right), pose by the "stand" where they sold soda and candy to those who came to swim and fish in the Poestenkill Creek at White Bridge. Mrs. Shippey also sold doilies she crocheted in her free time for 50¢ each. The Shippey family later replaced the stand with a gas station, now destroyed. In 1935, a son, Harold, opened an automobile racetrack called The Clear View, a short-lived enterprise. (From the album of the late Donald E. Hall.)

SPIAK'S SERVICE TRUCK, SPIAK'S GARAGE, 1165 HOOSICK ROAD (ROUTE 7), 1939. James "Mickey" Spiak Sr. (see p. 58) opened a garage and gas station about 1934. His service truck was parked near the Socony gas pumps when photographed. The license plate reveals the date of picture, 1939, when the World's Fair was held in New York City. This business is now operated by Mickey's son, James Jr. (Courtesy Cora Spiak.)

LOOKING TOWARD WEEDEN'S GARAGE AND THE GARFIELD SCHOOL FROM THE EAGLE MILLS CEMETERY, BRUNSWICK ROAD (ROUTE 2), EAGLE MILLS. Harold Weeden opened this gas station and garage about 1930. The business was acquired by Clarence Freckleton about 1956 and is presently operated by Gordon Christian. The rear addition to the Garfield School (see p. 6), added to accommodate sanitary facilities, can be seen here. (Photograph by John E. Lynd; courtesy Marion Lynd.)

THE NEW YORK STATE POLICE TROOP G HEADQUARTERS, SOUTH LAKE AVENUE, C. 1926. Eighty-one members of Troop G moved into their new headquarters on April 21, 1921. The design of the building was adapted from a similar one in Oneida, New York. A stable for horses used by the mounted police also occupied the site. Troop G vacated the facility in 1959 and established a new post in Loudonville. This facility is now used by the New York Army National Guard. (Town of Brunswick Collection.)

THE COUNTRY CLUB OF TROY, 1929. The Country Club of Troy was incorporated in 1925 and purchased 170 acres of undeveloped land from the then financially struggling Forest Hills Cemetery, formerly Forest Park Cemetery (see p. 87), as well as adjacent farmland. The club opened in 1927 and offered a golf course, tennis courts, swimming pool, and clubhouse. The golf course, recognized as one of the area's finest, was designed by Walter J. Travis, the first American to win the British Amateur Championship (1904) and a prominent course architect and player. (Courtesy Country Club of Troy.)

A HORSE SHOW SPONSORED BY THE TROY HORSE SHOW ASSOCIATION, BRUNSWICK ROAD (ROUTE 2), NEAR PRESENT-DAY RIDING CLUB ROAD. From 1919 until about 1940 the Troy Horse Show Association sponsored an annual horse show that enjoyed a national reputation for outstanding exhibition and competition. Franklin and Eleanor Roosevelt attended several times. The shows came to an end with the passing of the founders and original supporters of the Troy Horse Show Association. (Courtesy Mr. and Mrs. Don Hurley.)

JIM POWERS ON HORSEBACK, PINEWOODS RIDING ACADEMY, PINEWOODS AVENUE NEAR THE FOREST PARK CEMETERY ENTRANCE, c. 1935. The Pinewoods Riding Academy was owned by Charles Crowley, who lived on Belle Avenue in Troy. This photograph looks west toward the stable. Banbury Road now occupies land once associated with the academy, which ceased operations during World War II. (Courtesy Pauline Palladino and Mr. and Mrs. George Reckner.)

THE FOREST PARK CEMETERY, LATER FOREST HILLS CEMETERY, PINEWOODS AVENUE, ORIGINALLY DEVELOPED 1897, C. 1900. The organizers of the Forest Park Cemetery engaged the services of Garnet D. Baltimore, the first African American to graduate from Rensselaer Polytechnic Institute (1881), to develop a design for a 200-acre cemetery. Pictured are the only features of Baltimore's elaborate design ever realized as the corporation soon went bankrupt. A second incorporation as Forest Hills Cemetery also failed during the 1930s. Without a governing body, the cemetery was ravaged by Mother Nature and vandals before management of the cemetery was assumed by the Town of Brunswick in 1990, in accordance with the municipal laws of New York State. (Town of Brunswick Collection.)

THE RUFUS H. SAGE MAUSOLEUM, BRUNSWICK CEMETERY, ROUTE 278. Rufus H. Sage was the nephew of Russell Sage, the Troy merchant turned Wall Street financier, and the son of Henry and Catherine Sage. He, along with his wife, Ellen, and a brother, Russell Sage Jr., are interred in this mausoleum. Russell Sage Jr.'s given name was Russell Sage II. (Photograph by Sharon Martin Zankel.)

THE POPLAR TERRACE TOURIST HOME, HOOSICK ROAD (ROUTE 7), CENTER BRUNSWICK, c. 1940. Just as the stagecoaches of the 19th century had encouraged the erection of several hotels along the Hoosick Road, the ease of automobile travel in the 1930s and 1940s resulted in the establishment of tourist homes along this thoroughfare. Families with extra bedrooms welcomed overnight guests; some provided meals. The Wagner family operated this tourist home. (Brunswick Historical Society Collection.)

PLEASANT VIEW CABINS, ROUTE 7 NEAR INTERSECTION WITH CARROLLS GROVE ROAD, c. 1930. Operated by Herbert and Queenie Bulson, these accommodations offered "showers, hot and cold water in every cabin, and flush toilets." This picture is from a postcard. (Courtesy Michael Coffey.)

BENTLEY'S RESTAURANT AND BAR, CLUM'S CORNERS, AT THE INTERSECTION OF ROUTE 278 AND TAMARAC ROAD, C. 1940. Commonly referred to as "B's," this establishment offered casual dining. Pictured from left to right are chef "Big Bill," Alice Bentley, owner Hiram Bentley, and Claude Bentley, a cousin. The business was previously operated as Freemont's and before that as the Green Parrot Dance Hall by Sam McChesney. A sign for Winne's ice cream (see p. 91), made in Eagle Mills, can be seen to the left. A Stewart's Shop now stands on the site of this business. (From the album of the late A. Frank Bentley.)

THE CHAINED BEAR, CLUM'S CORNERS. Printed from a postcard, this photograph features a chained bear associated with a business known as the Canary Bird Tea Room at Clum's Corners. It has been said the Bentley family, and the Freemonts before them, kept a chained bear at the Clum's Corners establishment, but no one recalls either family operating under the name Canary Bird Tea Room. (Courtesy Florence Grabo.)

HAPPY DEAN'S BAND AT THE OLD HEIDELBERG, CREEK ROAD, C. 1937. The musicians pictured are, from left to right, Happy Dean, Harold Wheeler, Elmer Milhizer, George Forman, Joe Koenerbauer, and Mike Tcinsky. This band was one of many that played at the Old Heidelberg, an enterprise founded by Bill Rowe (see p. 42) in the 1920s. This well-known nightclub, consisting of a dance floor with a bar "in the back," experienced two fires in its history; the last fire, in the early 1950s, brought the business to a close. (Courtesy Elmer Milhizer.)

ANDREW'S RESTAURANT, 665 BRUNSWICK ROAD (ROUTE 2), EAST OF EAGLE MILLS, 1977. Linda Grissom Swift posed outside Andrew's Restaurant on the occasion of her wedding dinner. This popular restaurant was owned by Andrew and Steven Triantefillou. Before that it was operated for 23 years as the Hollis Tea Room by C.J. Hollis. In 1978, the building was sold to the Brunswick Lodge of Elks No. 2256. The Elks expanded the building to include a meeting and banquet facility. (Courtesy Jeanne Butler Jarrett.)

BROWN'S GARAGE, ROUTE 2, CLUM'S CORNERS. In 1933 Leon Brown opened an automotive repair service and about 1939 began dealing in Ford-Ferguson tractors. The dealership grew to be one of the largest in the area. Sometime after "Brownie," as Leon was known, passed away, it was acquired by Tom Joyce who renamed it Alpine Tractor. Today King Fuels occupies the site. (Courtesy Bill Brown.)

EAGLE MILLS CREAMERY, BRUNSWICK ROAD (ROUTE 2), EAST OF THE EAGLE MILLS BRIDGE. The Eagle Mills Creamery, behind the old Eagle Mills Hotel, was founded by Harold J. Winne around 1929 and he operated it until about 1967. Ice cream, butter, and cottage cheese were among the best-selling products. The creamery was later used as an auto parts store but is presently vacant. (Brunswick Historical Society Collection.)

HOWE BROTHERS, HOOSICK ROAD (ROUTE 7) AT GRANGE ROAD (ROUTE 142). Howe Brothers was founded by John Howe and was originally located in Troy. After a fire destroyed that facility, the business was reestablished in Brunswick about 1920. John Howe became acquainted with a fellow named Coleman, who had designed a four-wheel drive, heavy-duty truck to which he gave his name. Declining the offer of a partnership with Coleman, John Howe merely sold the Coleman trucks, eventually redesigned the Coleman's front end, and patented it as the Howe-Coleman. Pictured are Howe Brothers' first Brunswick garage and early Coleman trucks with snowplows. The business today is operated by John's son Frank and John's grandsons, Wayne and Ned. (Courtesy Frank Howe.)

JALOPY RACING, CARROLLS GROVE, CARROLLS GROVE ROAD, OFF ROUTE 7 BETWEEN CENTER BRUNSWICK AND HAYNERSVILLE. For more than 20 years, Bernard Carroll and his family offered folks from the surrounding area several varieties of entertainment at their grove. While clamsteams and dance music were the most enduring attractions, jalopy racing and an animal park proved briefly successful. The business ended in 1966. (Courtesy Mr. and Mrs. Carl O'Brien.)

THE BRUNSWICK SUPER MARKET, HOOSICK ROAD (ROUTE 7). In the 1940s, Benjamin "Berke" Ginsburg and his wife, Anna Stone (see p. 102), founded the Brunswick Super Market. Following Berke's death in 1967, his son, Sonny Ginsburg, and his son's wife, Jean, operated the business. The business closed a few years after Sonny's passing in 1977. Members of the Ginsburg family now operate Brunswick Harley-Davidson at this location. (Courtesy Ginsburg Family.)

RIFENBURG'S GENERAL MERCHANDISE, ROUTE 2, CROPSEYVILLE, C. 1930. Formerly the Pleasant Valley store (see p. 27), Charles H. Rifenburg acquired the business in 1905. It was a popular general store where youngsters lined up to be weighed on the grain scale. Charles's son Earl and Earl's wife, Edna, converted it to a self-service market in 1955. Many remember Earl kept a pet trout in an old watering trough; it grew to 2 feet in length in two years because he fed it cat food. In 1970 the Rifenburgs retired from the business. Peter Coyne operated the store briefly thereafter. It now serves as a residence. (Brunswick Historical Society Collection.)

THE STONE QUARRY OWNED AND OPERATED BY CALLANAN INDUSTRIES, ROUTE 2, EAST OF CROPSEYVILLE AT THE BRUNSWICK-GRAFTON TOWN LINE. The quarry land essentially includes Camel Mountain and several adjacent properties. It was developed and first operated by the Fitzgerald Brothers Construction Company of Troy, who opened the plant in 1951. The quarry is a major supplier of crushed stone for Rensselaer County and the surrounding area. An asphalt plant was added in 1957. (Courtesy Callanan Industries.)

Seven
FRIENDS AND NEIGHBORS

THE HIRAM WAGAR FAMILY, EAGLE MILLS. Seated in front in this scene are Hiram Wagar and his wife, Gitty Ann Trumble. In the back are the Wagar children; from left to right are Clint, Elleda, and Leddra. Mr. Wagar lost his arm in the Battle at Hatcher's Run during the Civil War. The home pictured was that of Leslie and Bertha Clum, on Brunswick Road near the intersection of Maple Avenue, Eagle Mills. Photographs of family and friends are among people's most cherished possessions. Just as a family might compile an album of its generations, so should a community preserve the images of its citizens, for it is the people who perpetuate the sense of community. (Brunswick Historical Society Collection.)

JOSEPH H. HIDLEY
(1830–1872), ARTIST, HOUSE
PAINTER, TAXIDERMIST, AND
FLORAL ARRANGER. This
photograph was produced from
a tintype. Hidley was born in
what is now North Greenbush.
His father died when he was
four years old and his mother
married William W. Coonradt
of Brunswick. Hidley is best
known in Brunswick for scenes
he painted on window and
fireplace panels in several area
homes. He produced several
landscape paintings of
neighboring towns
but none depicting Brunswick
have ever been found. (New
York State Library,
Manuscripts and Special
Collections.)

JULIETTE HUBBARD NEWBURY, EARLY
CROPSEYVILLE RESIDENT. Juliette was
born in the early 1800s before New
York laws, enacted in 1880, required
the keeping of vital statistics such as
birth, marriage, and death dates.
Juliette was the grandmother of M.
Louise Newbury (see p. 75). Her home
appears on p. 24. (Courtesy Robert
Newbury.)

PEARL WOODIN POTTER (1873–1934).
Pearl lived in Eagle Mills. Her husband, J. Howard Potter (1872–1945), was named Brunswick Town Clerk in 1908 upon the resignation of W.H. Finkle. Mr. Potter's first official act was to appoint Pearl deputy town clerk, making her Brunswick's first woman official. Pearl was later appointed "local historian" in 1920, at an annual salary of $50. Pearl was the mother of Guy Potter. (Town of Brunswick Collection.)

HENRIETTA MOODY MILLER. Henrietta and her husband, John, operated an undertaking business in Eagle Mills beginning in the late 19th century. Account books maintained by the Millers indicate they charged $5 for embalming the body of the deceased. It has been said Henrietta created a striking image when driving about with her horse and buggy. (Courtesy Irene Miller.)

ANDREW MULLIN (1844–1913). Andrew lived in Eagle Mills, where he manufactured cigars, kept a store, and served as postmaster. He served as Brunswick Town Clerk from 1879 to 1907 (except 1882 to 1884). Here he is pictured in his store (see p. 20). Andrew enjoyed photography and several photographs attributed to him appear in this collection. He was the husband of Sarah Allen (see p. 56) and the father of Florence Mullin (Reed), who also served as town clerk (see p. 16). The unusual work on the next page was created by Andrew. (Town of Brunswick Collection.)

CHARLES BUTLER, PROBABLY IN THE YARD OF HIS HOME ON CREEK ROAD. Charles operated a barbershop in the Eagle Mills store during the 1930s and worked as a janitor at the Garfield School. As may be guessed from this photograph, Charles enjoyed gardening, often doing work for others. (Brunswick Historical Society Collection.)

In Memoriam.

Born

JULY 19th 1845.

Died

APRIL 10th 1899.

Hon. Richard A. Derrick,

Served the Town as Justice of the Peace, from January 1st 1879
to December 31st 1882 and from Jany 1st 1887 to Nov. 10th 1887 and
as Supervisor from Nov. 10th 1887 continuously
to April 10th 1899.

Resolutions Adopted by the Town Board;

Whereas, In the providence of Almighty God, our esteemed friend and townsman Hon. Richard A. Derrik, late Supervisor of the town of Brunswick, and Presiding Officer of this board, was on the 10th day of April past removed by death. Therefore be it

Resolved, That we, as a board deeply regret our loss, and shall greatly miss his genial presence and wise counsels.

Resolved, That the sympathy of this board be extended to his bereaved family, and that a copy of these Resolutions be sent to the family, and a page in the Town Records be Dedicated to his memory.

Resolved, That in adopting these Resolutions we as a board believe that we voice the sentiments of the town at large.

Thomas H. Betts,

RICHARD A. DERRICK (1843–1899). This image of a well-known Brunswick public servant survives in the records of the Town of Brunswick and was created and preserved by Town Clerk Andrew Mullin. The son of Richard C. and Johanna M. Derrick, Richard was appointed postmaster of Brunswick by Abraham Lincoln in 1861. He served in the New York State Assembly two terms, was president of the Society for Apprehending Horse Thieves, and was a census enumerator. At the time of his death he was serving as Brunswick Town Supervisor, an office he held from 1888 to 1899. Richard lived in Center Brunswick (see p. 35) with his wife, Augusta Tuttle. (Courtesy Brunswick Town Clerk.)

EDWARD SULLY PICKERING (1887–1930) AND HIS WIFE, ANNA L. NOLAN (1886–1972), C. 1913. Mr. and Mrs. Pickering operated Lowland Grove, a produce farm at the end of what is today Taylor Lane. The farm was founded by Edward's grandmother, Anne Webster Campbell Pickering, who came here from England c. 1846. Edward carted vegetables to the Troy Public Market six days a week and was known to pay his workers for a 60-hour workweek, although he only required 59 hours of work! After Edward died, Anna sold the farm to then-Congressman Dean Taylor, who razed most of the buildings for residential construction. (Courtesy Edward J. Pickering.)

DR. THEODORE ST. JOHN AND FAMILY, CENTER BRUNSWICK, C. 1910. Dr. St. John practiced medicine in Brunswick for 46 years; upon his death in 1922 at the age of 74, he was cited as the oldest living graduate of Albany Medical College. From left to right, these members of the St. John family, pictured at their home, are the doctor's wife, Caroline Filkens; daughter-in-law Mae Kavanaugh St. John; daughter Olive (Film); daughter Mary (Davidson), who is holding her niece, Mary Caroline (daughter of Mae); and Dr. St. John himself. (Courtesy Carolyn Film Edwards.)

ROBERT DUNCAN OF CROPSEYVILLE, WORLD WAR I SOLDIER. Robert, the son of Daniel and Adelia Bulson Dunham, served in the 311th Infantry, Machine Gun Company. In a letter written in 1918 while training at Fort Dix, New Jersey, he said the camp had "24 miles of trench, dugouts, and barbed wire entanglements for drill purposes." He shipped out, fought in Europe, and returned to Cropseyville. (Courtesy Mildred McChesney.)

CLARENCE F. "POP" STARKS (1879–1974) AND HIS RACEHORSE, C. 1940. Pop Starks operated a store in Center Brunswick on the Hoosick Road west of Route 278. He sold groceries, household goods, and hardware. It has been said you could always tell when Pop was going to race his horse at the Saratoga track because he would have on his suit. This photograph was taken behind the store. (Courtesy Cora Spiak.)

JOE COONRAD PUMPING GAS AT HIS CENTER BRUNSWICK GARAGE, C. 1940. Joe Coonrad learned the blacksmith's trade as a young man (see p. 11) and, when cars came along, learned to work on Ford engines. On Independence Day, Joe would put on a stovepipe hat and march in the parade. This photograph was taken by Mary Dusenberry, who lived on Dusenberry Lane and frequently "stopped by Joe's garage." (Courtesy Mary Dusenberry.)

BENJAMIN "BERKE" GINSBURG AND WIFE, ANNA STONE. This picture was probably taken in Troy. Mr. Ginsburg was nicknamed Berke and known also as "The Turkey King." A Troy cattle dealer, Ben started raising great numbers of turkeys after he moved to Brunswick. Ben and Anna operated the Brunswick Super Market (see p. 93) on Hoosick Road west of Pop Starks's place. (Courtesy Ginsburg Family.)

A 1940s Brunswick Highway Crew.
George Grabo (right) was elected
Brunswick Highway Superintendent in
1941 and served until his retirement in
1958. George supervised a crew of eight
men, two of whom are pictured here. Carl
Bulson is in the center and Aubrey
Stannard is on the left; George always
called Aubrey his "right-hand man."
(Courtesy Florence Grabo.)

Samuel and Mabel Miller,
photographed in the 1940s. Sam and
Mabel Miller owned the Fertile Valley
Farm on Church Street (see p. 65). Sam
served as town supervisor from 1948 to
1950. Upon Sam's sudden death in 1950,
the Brunswick Town Board appointed
Mabel to fill his post; she served through
December 31, 1951. They had two
children, Warren and Jean. (Courtesy
Jean Miller.)

A MOCK WEDDING—A CELEBRATION OF MR. AND MRS. ALARIE'S 25TH WEDDING ANNIVERSARY, 1946. Timothy and Albena Alarie celebrated their "silver" wedding anniversary on New Year's Eve by staging a mock wedding with their Mountain View friends and neighbors. Seated in front of the bride and groom are Laura Allen (left) and Mary Sturgeon. In the back are Ceina Deutsch, Fred Lavrin, Lucy Jarry, and Alice Morand. Tim and Albena were active in the Mountain View Fire Department and Ladies Auxiliary, as were several that celebrated with them. (Courtesy Iva Riordan.)

BRUNSWICK RED CROSS VOLUNTEERS KATHLEEN BENTLEY (LEFT) AND LOIS VOGT (RIGHT) AT ALBANY MEDICAL CENTER WITH YOUNG PATIENTS. Volunteer work and community association encouraged a close friendship between Kathleen and Lois. When Kathleen died in 1968, Lois drove the Red Cross's station wagon in the funeral procession. Lois served as a Red Cross volunteer for 40 years. (From the album of the late A. Frank Bentley.)

RAY EATON OF BRUNSWICK PERFORMING LIVE ON TELEVISION, C. 1956. This photograph was taken at the Menands studio of station WAST, now WNYT, Channel 13. WNYT first went on the air as WTRI, broadcasting from a studio on Bald Mountain, in 1954. Here, Ray, standing to the right in a plaid shirt, appears on a live country-music show hosted by Hiram Hopps (Fred Shavor), left. Ray maintained the station's transmitters on Bald Mountain for almost 40 years. (Courtesy Fred Shavor.)

LOUIS MILLER (C. 1907–1990), OWNER OF MILLER'S SERVICE AND SUPPLY, 901 HOOSICK ROAD (ROUTE 7), C. 1950. Lou Miller and his wife, Veronica (below), operated an appliance and lawnmower sales and service business from a garage in back of their home for over 50 years, closing the business in 1988. (From the album of the late Veronica Miller.)

VERONICA "PAL" MILLER (1910–1998), PHOTOGRAPHED IN 1954 BEHIND THE COUNTER OF MILLER'S SERVICE AND SUPPLY. Pal assisted her husband in the operation of their business by selling parts and paint and helping with the repair of lawn mowers. Lou made the shelves pictured behind Pal from oak boxes used to ship pumps during World War II. (From the album of the late Veronica Miller.)

SANFORD L. CLUETT (1875–1968). Sanford patented "sanforization," the process that prevented textiles from shrinking more than one percent. He lived in the home built by Charles Betts *c.* 1919, east of The Crossway on Spring Avenue, and graduated from Rensselaer Polytechnic Institute in 1899. As vice-president of Cluett, Peabody, and Co., Inc., he continued to revolutionize the textile industry, holding more than two hundred patents by the end of his career. (Courtesy Rensselaer County Historical Society.)

TELEVISION CELEBRITY "MR. FOOD," ART GINSBURG. Born in Troy, Art moved to Horton Avenue in Brunswick with his family in 1970. He started a catering business about the same time he began to perform with a local theatrical group. A guest appearance on a television talk show led to regular appearances, then his own show on station WRGB, and eventually, national syndication. Art decided to call himself "Mr. Food," and coined his famous line "Ooh, it's so good!" while residing in Brunswick. He now lives in Florida. (Courtesy Art Ginsburg.)

R. JOHN DUNCAN (1910–1997) AND HIS WIFE, RUTH KELLER DUNCAN (1910–1989), OWNERS AND OPERATORS OF DUNCAN'S DAIRY BAR, 890 HOOSICK ROAD (ROUTE 7). Brunswick's longest-operating eatery was established by John and Ruth in 1939. The Duncans initially sold ice cream and eventually developed a full dinner menu. Homemade bread, doughnuts, muffins, and pies, along with the Duncan's friendly service, made their business successful. The restaurant is now operated by the Duncan's children and grandchildren. (Courtesy Duncan Family.)

BRUNSWICK POLITICAL FIGURES FRANK MCKNIGHT AND JOE BRUNO AT A LINCOLN DAY DINNER, MARIO'S THEATRE RESTAURANT, TROY, 1971. Assemblyman Neil Kelleher (left) and Donald Wickham, commissioner of the department of agriculture and markets, posed with Francis "Frank" McKnight (second from right) and Joseph L. "Joe" Bruno (right) for photographer Jack Short. Frank has served as Brunswick Town Supervisor (1952–1957) and as a town justice since 1965. Joe Bruno, at the time of this photograph, was assistant to Assembly Speaker Perry Duryea. In 1976, Joe was elected to the New York State Senate. He has continued to represent Brunswick in the senate, achieving the office of senate majority leader in 1995. This photograph appeared in *The Record*, February 13, 1971. (Town of Brunswick Collection.)

Eight
A COUNTRY LIFE

THE MILTZ FARM, BALD MOUNTAIN, C. 1910. John Miltz and wife, Gertrude, seem distracted by an out-of-the-scene occurrence while daughter Marion and the team, Polly and Daisy, posed for the photographer. John is standing on a stone boat, an implement used to haul stones picked up while clearing fields for planting. His German-born parents, Joseph and Maria Miltz, purchased the farm about 1870. Three generations of the Miltz family shared the farmhouse. John hired on as a snow shoveler with the town in the winter earning 25¢ an hour. Diversion from the daily routine came in the form of neighborly visits, occasional trips "to town" for necessities, and church activities. (Courtesy Florence Grabo.)

A DUTCH-STYLE BARN, BUILT C. 1774, FORMERLY ON THE WAGNER FARM, GARFIELD ROAD. Several New World Dutch barns may be found in Brunswick. This barn was unusually large for an 18th-century barn, measuring about 50 feet wide and 60 feet long. The construction of these barns is distinguished by the use of H-frame supports, a feature that accounts for their strength and endurance. This barn was taken down in 1996 and has been rebuilt near Weston, Vermont. (Photograph by Peter Sinclair.)

A BARN AND A C. 1916 TILE SILO ON THE JOHN TARBOX FARM, ROUTE 7 BETWEEN CENTER BRUNSWICK AND HAYNERSVILLE. Once part of John Melchoir File's property (see p. 35), this farm was acquired by George F. Tarbox in 1944 and is now operated by George's son John and George's grandson, David. The heart of the main barn is a c. 1800 Dutch barn, now expanded. Tile silos are rare in this area. (Courtesy John and Joann Tarbox.)

DAVID ANSON SMITH'S BLACKSMITH SHOP, HOOSICK ROAD (ROUTE 7) AT INTERSECTION OF GRANGE ROAD (ROUTE 142), 1887. There may have been as many blacksmith shops in Brunswick one hundred years ago as there are gas stations today but none were self-service. The smithy shod horses and oxen; some created iron hardware and other implements. It was a place where men congregated to visit and one where children found entertainment watching the smithy forge iron into horseshoes. (Town of Brunswick Collection.)

THE CONSTITUTION OF THE BRUNSWICK SOCIETY FOR APPREHENDING HORSE AND CHICKEN THIEVES. In Brunswick's early days, when almost every household kept one or more horses and a flock of chickens, the theft of these beasts caused inconvenience, if not hardship. This organization provided its members about 50 percent reimbursement for the value of the lost animal and a reward for those who recovered the animal. The organization first met in 1823 and continued meeting through the early 1900s. (Brunswick Historical Society Collection.)

THE FARMHOUSE ASSOCIATED WITH THE ELM PLACE DAIRY, GRANGE ROAD (ROUTE 142) AT THE INTERSECTION OF NORTH LAKE AVENUE, C. 1900. The Elm Place Dairy was operated by several generations of the Abbott family in the 19th century. This photograph is from a postcard. The property was later owned by Lindy. Most of the barns and outbuildings associated with the property have burned or been removed. (Courtesy Michael Branigan.)

FOUR GENERATIONS OF THE ABBOTT FAMILY. Seen in this c. 1903 photograph are, from left to right, Ira Willard Abbott (born 1851); Ira's grandchild, Willard Abbott (born 1902), Richard's son; Ira's son, Richard Waldo Abbott (born 1878); and Ira's father, Henry Judd Abbott (born 1819). Henry, Ira, and Richard were the operators of the Elm Place Dairy. (Courtesy Don T. Birkmayer.)

RICHARD WALDO ABBOTT DRIVING THE ELM PLACE DAIRY MILK DELIVERY WAGON, C. 1899. The vehicle featured canvas shades that could be rolled down to keep the sun from warming the metal milk cans. The delivery man may have carried a bell that he would ring to let people know he was outside the door; they would then bring out a milk container that the delivery man filled by scooping milk from the large cans with a dipper. (Courtesy Don T. Birkmayer.)

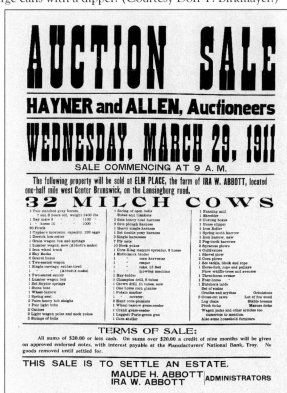

AN ELM PLACE AUCTION BROADSIDE. Broadsides, or notices, such as this were posted in public places to advertise an event. Following the early death of Richard Waldo Abbott, the family decided to sell Elm Place. A study of the broadside reveals the types of equipment and implements used on a Brunswick farm. Note the spelling of the word milk. (Courtesy Don T. Birkmayer.)

THE BRUNSWICK CREAMERY OFF PRESENT MOONLAWN ROAD, EAGLE MILLS, 1897. Operated by Louis Thurston, the Brunswick Creamery purchased milk from farmers for the production of dairy products such as butter and cottage cheese. These products were then sold to milkmen, who had established routes and sold the products to their customers by home delivery. A dairymen's league encouraged ethical practices among milkmen. For example, if one sold his route to another, he could not establish another route for at least a year. This creamery had an apartment upstairs, occupied at the time by the Elmer Miller family. Emma Mayer Miller is holding her baby daughter, Ethel (see p. 46). Alvah Carner later purchased the creamery and, about 1910, erected a new building at 25 Moonlawn Road that housed the Brunswick Creamery and Produce Company. (Town of Brunswick Collection.)

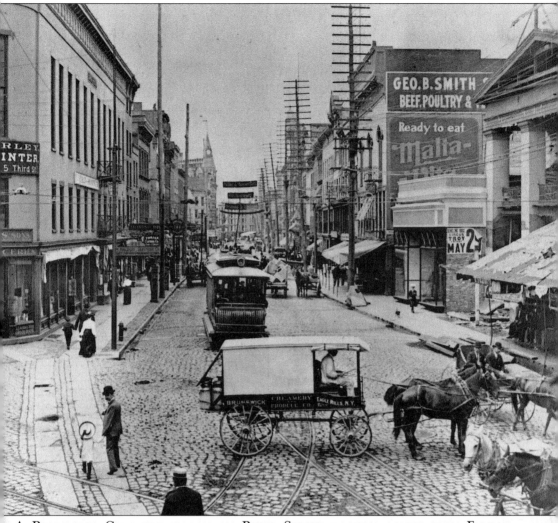

A Brunswick Creamery wagon on River Street looking south from Fulton Street, Troy, c. 1890. The nearby city of Troy provided Brunswick's farmers a lucrative market for dairy products, fresh produce, hay, and other agricultural products. The building with columns to the right was the Fulton Market. The building advertising Smith's Poultry was the Odd Fellows Hall. "Going to the city" meant a trip to Troy to conduct business as well as shop at Troy's many department stores. (Courtesy Rensselaer County Historical Society.)

CLARISSA HULBERT, CROPSEYVILLE, 1902. Most Brunswick families kept a few chickens in the backyard; eggs as well as the birds were consumed. Extra eggs were sold to supplement the family's income. Mrs. Hulbert is wearing a bonnet, probably homemade, that featured a rear cape to protect one's neck and shoulders from the sun. (Courtesy Iola Simmons.)

DORA KEYES SELLING EGGS AND GARDEN PRODUCE AT HER HOME AT 936 HOOSICK ROAD (ROUTE 7), 1950s. Automobile travelers along Routes 2 and 7 have long enjoyed stopping at Brunswick's roadside stands. While few, if any, Brunswick families today keep chickens and sell eggs, fresh produce may be found for sale at roadside stands around the town. (Courtesy Doris Shaffer.)

PLOWING ON THE POLLOCK FARM, PENNYROYAL LANE, C. 1910. Pictured is Philip Pierce Pollock plowing on the farm owned by his father, Franklin Pierce Pollock. The property served five generations of the Pollock family before it was sold and divided. Norton Miller, a botanist who has erected a new home on a part of the farm, recently discovered a rare liverwort, *frullania bolanderi*, growing on ancient trees on this farm, the only place it is known in New York state. (Courtesy Phil Pollock.)

A BRUNSWICK BARNYARD, 1926. It is believed this photograph was taken on the property now owned by the Dunham family on Dater Hill Road. It was formerly the Shyne Farm and the photograph is attributed to John Devine. These cows have horns. Today a cow's horns are removed shortly after birth or the animals are bred as polled (hornless) cows. (Courtesy Barbara Hewitt.)

"Josie" and "Billy," raised in Center Brunswick, 1921. These porkers were named for Will Draffin and Joe Coonrad. They were slaughtered on November 15, 1921. Josie weighed 198 pounds and Billy 209 pounds. Most Brunswick farms raised one or more pigs for the family's meat supply. (Brunswick Historical Society Collection.)

Harvested Oats, Elmer Miller's Farm, McChesney Avenue Extension, c. 1920. Ethel Miller's camera (see p. 46) captured this field of shocked oats on her father's farm. The grain had to be well shocked after cutting. The perfect shock was one that would stand up in windy weather and provide the grain heads protection from the weather. (Courtesy Irene Miller.)

HAYING ON THE MITTELSTED FARM, MENEMSHA LANE, 1921. August and Mary Mittelsted acquired this farm in 1902 from the Kilmer family. Menemsha Lane was previously known as Mittelsted Road. At the time of this photograph the farm was operated by August's son, William Mittelsted, who may be the man on the hay wagon. Hay was used for bedding farm animals and was sold by the ton to Troy stables. The aroma of new mown hay yet fills the days of summer here in parts of Brunswick. (Courtesy Betsy Durivage.)

ICE HARVESTING ON THE PATTON FARM, PINEWOODS AVENUE, EARLY 1900S. Just as haying occupied much of the summer, ice harvesting was an essential winter chore. Blocks of ice were packed in sawdust and stored in icehouses for use during the warmer months. The Pattons cut ice for their own use and perhaps sold the excess to neighbors. (Courtesy Donald Patton.)

SWIMMING IN THE POESTENKILL CREEK, C. 1920. This happy group included, from left to right, Leslie Reckner, Will Reckner, Isetta Reckner Patton, Albert Reckner, Grace Reckner, and Rose Wagar. Brunswick's ponds and streams provided many convenient swimming holes. The Quackenkill and Poestenkill Creeks offered the most popular spots. Today, town residents may swim at the Brunswick Beach, opened in 1968 and operated by the Town of Brunswick. A few, however, still prefer to swim in the creeks. (Courtesy Donald Patton.)

SHOWING THE CITY FOLKS AROUND, MITTELSTED FARM, MAY 30, 1922. William Mittelsted (see p. 119) had a milk delivery route in Troy. During the summer, some of his customers, desiring a breath of country air, came and boarded at Mittelsted Farm. On this day, Mr. Mittelsted is giving his boarders a ride around the farm in his delivery wagon. (Courtesy Betsy Durivage.)

CORN CUTTING ON THE DUSENBERRY FARM, DUSENBERRY LANE OFF GRANGE ROAD (ROUTE 142), 1939. The help offered by friends and neighbors has always been one of a farmer's greatest assets. This group looks as if it put in a long but satisfying day. Pictured from left to right are Stanley Golinski, Will Tracy, unidentified, George Smith, Charles Wagner, and Harry Dusenberry, who owned the farm. Helpers were usually invited to stay for dinner. (Photograph by Mary Dusenberry.)

SHOOTING DARTS IN WALTER GOYER'S BARN, CROPSEYVILLE. Getting together for conversation and recreation has always helped one wind down after a day's work. Before health clubs were introduced, a corner of the barn was a good place to trade horse stories and shoot a few darts. Walter Goyer (center) is seen with Bill Rourke (right), who worked on the state road crew, and an unidentified man. (Brunswick Historical Society Collection.)

THOMAS PATTON (1880–1974), PLOWING WITH A MULE, C. 1930. Tom farmed and delivered milk. His day began at 3:00 a.m. with milking the cows. At the height of his milk delivery business, he sold 800 quarts of milk a day, delivered by a horse-drawn wagon to customers in Troy. After delivery of the milk, there were a multitude of chores to be done back on the farm as well as the evening milking. (Courtesy Donald Patton.)

WILL TRACY WITH HIS TEAM, "EMONS AND AMOS," ON THE DUSENBERRY FARM, 1941. Horses were used on most Brunswick farms through the late 1940s. While farmers did have tractors, not all the farm equipment was readily adaptable for hitching to a tractor. The advent of World War II also discouraged some farmers from giving up their horses. Gas rationing and a shortage of tires were of little concern to a farmer with a good team. (Photograph by Mary Dusenberry.)

WAGAR BROTHERS DAIRY, SPRING AVENUE, NOW OPERATED AS MOXIE'S. In 1897, Sylvanus and Christina Wagar purchased a farm on Spring Avenue. Later their sons, Elmer, Clifford, Clayton, and Freeman, operated milk routes in Troy. About 1933, the Wagar brothers, along with their brother-in-law, Lester Schumann, constructed a pasteurization plant across the road from the farm. An ice cream stand, added in 1938, became one of the most popular in the area. The business passed out of the Wagar family in 1964. (Courtesy Warren Rymiller.)

HOWARD WAGAR (1890–1952) AT HIS CENTER BRUNSWICK HOME ON HOOSICK ROAD. Howard was one of the founders of the Diamond Rock Creamery in Lansingburgh and was the Center Brunswick Volunteer Fire Company's first chief (he was not involved with the Wagar Brothers mentioned above). Howard was married to Edith Peckham (1889–1979), who had a twin sister named Ethel. (Courtesy Mr. and Mrs. Robert Hepp.)

EARL SHEFFER DRIVING CARRIAGE PULLED BY COWS "MARY" AND "MARIE," FOURTH OF JULY PARADE, CENTER BRUNSWICK, 1942. Mary and Marie were trained to pull a carriage when they were two months old. They were also used to rake hay and supplied milk and cream for the Sheffer family's table. In this scene, the Center Brunswick Methodist Church and manse are in the background. (Courtesy Edith Fichtner.)

THE SNYDER-HAYNER-FLOWER FARM, A NEW YORK CENTURY FARM, FLOWER ROAD, HAYNERSVILLE, NOW IVES'S MOUNTAIN GARDENS TREE FARM. This farm was among the first to be designated a Century Farm when the Order of Century Farmers was initiated by the New York State Agricultural Society in 1937. The program was established to recognize those farms that had been operated by successive generations of the same family for one hundred years or more. The farm was passed down through five generations of the Snyder family: John Lodewick Snyder, John George Snyder, John G. Snyder, Estella Snyder Hayner, and Ethna Hayner Flower. In 1946, the farm was purchased by Willard and Myrna Ives, who raise Christmas trees. (Brunswick Historical Society Collection.)

124

EDDIE ROBERTS WITH A CALF ON ROBERTS FARM, TAMARAC ROAD, 1952. Almost every youngster living on a farm raised a calf or other animal, sometimes as a 4-H project. This farm, formerly that of the Campbell family, was purchased by Francis Roberts in 1946; Francis said he remembered when the Tamarac Road was known as the Mud Turnpike and the hamlet of Tamarac was called Platestown because Peter Plates had operated a tavern there in the 1800s. (From the album of the late Francis Roberts.)

THE MILLER-HERRINGTON FARM, McCHESNEY AVENUE EXTENSION AT BONESTEEL LANE, c. 1955. Elmer Miller conveyed this farm to Harry and Jennie Herrington, who sold it to their son George in 1943. In 1958 George purchased the Brenenstuhl Farm on Tamarac Road and divided and sold this property. The barns and acreage were purchased by one party, and the house by another. No longer used, the barns pictured here today stand empty and silent, their presence adding a rustic flavor to the rural vista. (Courtesy Philip Herrington.)

RAY TRZCINSKI ON HIS JOHN DEERE 4010 TRACTOR AT THE TRZCINSKI FARM, CARROLLS GROVE ROAD. In 1923 Ray's parents, John and Theresa Trzcinski, purchased the farm he now operates. It was previously owned by the Shaver and Bishop families. Ray last used a team of horses to plow his fields in 1946. The Trzcinski farm is one of several dairy farms in operation in Brunswick today. Several farmers have turned to raising beef cattle or grain. (Courtesy Ray and Caroline Trzcinski.)

AN UPENDED FORD TRACTOR, 1953. George Reckner learned driving a tractor can sometimes be tricky on the day he tipped this tractor up on its rear end on his Pinewoods Avenue property. George said all he had to do to get it back to work was put a cable on it and pull it down. George was fortunate. Tractor accidents often have severe consequences. (Courtesy Mr. and Mrs. George Reckner.)

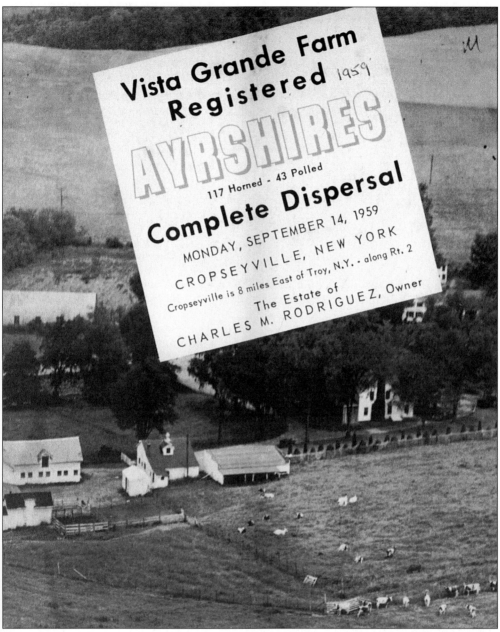

AN AUCTION CATALOG COVER FOR THE VISTA GRANDE FARM, OWNED BY CHARLES RODRIQUEZ, CROPSEYVILLE. About 1926 Charles Rodriquez, a native of Spain, purchased the property previously owned by the Clum, Betts, and Bornt families and founded the Vista Grande Farm. Rodriquez became a nationally recognized breeder of Ayshire cattle, winning numerous trophies throughout the United States. Charles served as president of both the Ayshire Breeders Association and Purebred Dairy Association before his death in 1959. Under several subsequent owners, Vista Grande has been operated as a horse farm. The Tamarac Plaza, Brunswick's first strip mall, was erected in 1969 on acreage once part of this farm. The view in the photograph looks toward Route 2 (obscured by a row of trees) from a hill in back of the farm. (Courtesy Harold Ashdown.)

THE CLUM-EDDY FARM, CLUM'S CORNERS, C. 1920. These children, standing by the farm's Packard truck, are, from left to right, Marion Eddy, H. Randall Eddy, and their cousin, Everett C. Eddy. This farm was owned by Sandford Clum, who grew potatoes for the commercial market. Later, his daughter Cora and her husband, Frank C. Eddy, owned the farm. Little did these youngsters realize the many changes the 20th century would bring to the farm, the community, and their lives! (Courtesy Eddy Family.)

DUNSHIRE FARM, PREVIOUSLY THE CLUM-EDDY FARM, LATER LANGMORE FARM, CLUM'S CORNERS, 1939. Horce Dunham purchased this farm in 1939 and named it Dunshire Farm. About 1944 it was acquired by Charles and Helen Moore who opened a dairy bar in the building pictured in the foreground. The Moores sold the farm structures and acreage in 1962 to Clinton J. Crandall, who created the housing development Tamarac View. Most of the buildings pictured no longer stand except for the barn on the right, which has hosted a number of business ventures. Images of our yesterdays stir the realization of the inevitable change that surrounds us! (Courtesy Brunswick Historical Society.)